Strength for the Walking Wounded

To my good friend —
Archbishop John Booch;
Dick Matheson was a wonder-
ful person and an outstanding
clergyman. I would guess you
met or came to know him during
both of your travels. I hope/know
you will enjoy some of his
fine messages!

Sincerely,
Warren Sawaras
Feb. 1985

STRENGTH FOR THE WALKING WOUNDED

Explorations in Faith

Richard Mathison

Burgess Publishing Company
Minneapolis, Minnesota

Acknowledgements

Richard Mathison gathered this sermon series together with the intention of publication. They are presented here in his memory, for the enrichment of all those whose lives he inspired, and also for those who missed the privilege of hearing him speak.

I wish to express my deep personal appreciation to all those friends whose encouragement and help have made this book possible. I am particularly grateful to Betty Cornwell, who not only typed the manuscript, but who helped every step of the way in readying this manuscript for publication.

Barbara Mathison

Richard P. Mathison was born October 17, 1931, in Eau Claire, Wisconsin. He graduated from the University of Minnesota and received his Master of Divinity degree from Yale Divinity School.

A member of the Minnesota Conference of the United Methodist Church, Richard Mathison served four churches in his twenty-six year ministry: Faith United Methodist Church in Minneapolis, Aurora-Hoyt Lakes United Methodist Church, University Methodist Church in Duluth (where he also served as Wesley Foundation Director), and Lake Harriet United Methodist Church in Minneapolis.

Richard Mathison died on August 18, 1979, in his 47th year.

This collection of sermons is dedicated
to the author's four children—
Mark, *Peter*, *Doug*, and *Becky*.

Contents

Introduction xi

Strength for the Walking Wounded 1

EXPLORING SOME
FOUNDATIONS OF FAITH

God: From Whom All Blessings Flow 9

Christ: God in His Fulness and Man at His Highest 14

Persons: Something Straight from God 19

The Church: A People on the March 24

The Bible: The Book One Always Comes Back To 30

EXPLORING SOME
HARD QUESTIONS OF FAITH

Take It To the Lord in Prayer 39
  (Does prayer do any good?)

Everest and Chimborazo 45
  (What do I do when I don't succeed?)

Established in the Faith 51
  (Can you give the Christian family some guidelines?)

Forgiveness as a Style of Life 57
  (How far does forgiveness go? If I am forgiven, am
  I also held responsible?)

You Pack Your Own Chute 63
   (Can faith help rearrange my life? When I try to
   improve, why do the negative aspects intensify?)

In Defense of Some Old-Fashioned Ideas 68
   (Does the Christian have something to say about
   sex, love, and marriage?)

He Who Comes in the Name of the Lord 74
   A Sermon for Palm Sunday (Is Jesus essential?
   What about other religions?)

Because He Lives! A Sermon for Easter Sunday 79
   (Is there life after death?)

CONCLUSION

God Is God, No Matter What 87

Introduction

In twenty-six years of ministry Richard Mathison preached nearly 1500 sermons. Like snowflakes, his sermons were crystalline, reflecting the light of God's creation, revelation and love to his congregations. And like snowflakes, no two were ever alike.

Preaching for Dick Mathison was an exciting and awesome calling, the focal point of his ministry. With each sermon he sought to unite the Word of God with the profound needs and hard questions of his congregation. "Let the words of my mouth and the meditation of our hearts be acceptable in thy sight" was a common preface to his sermons. Karl Barth wrote of his own preaching, "I sought to find my way between the problem of human life on the one hand and the content of the Bible on the other." Like Barth, Dick Mathison preached with the Bible and the daily newspaper side by side. God's living Word frequently emerged from the front page headlines, but just as frequently emerged from the sports section, the want ads, Dear Abby, Erma Bombeck, and Peanuts.

Through his preaching, Dick helped us see relationships that otherwise might have passed unnoticed. Beyond the newspaper, the Word of God was further revealed in blueberry bushes and baseball games, freeways and country roads, sculpture and architecture, advertisements and advent candles, hymns and happenings, situation comedies and serious documentaries, structure and spontaneity, the mysterious and the mundane, and ultimately life and death.

Timely and timeless, his sermons stimulated our imaginations and pricked our consciences. Each Sunday morning he helped us explore, dream, cope, care, believe, hope, sort out and carry on. Through his sermons, he taught us not so much what to think, but *how to think* about our faith, and how to celebrate it.

Dick Mathison used a fountain pen flowing with bright, green ink to write most of his sermon notes. No one seems to know why, except that green is the color of growth and flowing the process of life. No one affirmed growth and life in all its dimensions more than Dick Mathison did. The fifteen sermons in this collection are evidence of that.

Gil Kinnunen
A member of his congregation

Strength for the Walking Wounded

The Book of Job, especially chapters 3, 7, 38 and 42; John 16:33

In the year 1888, George Eastman brought out the first "Kodak" camera. It could use his newly-invented roll film. For the first time, as a little biographical sketch about Eastman puts it, the average person had "a language for recording what was true, and sometimes what was beautiful."[1]

I invite you to recall a piece of Christian good news, both true and beautiful: *there is strength for the walking wounded.*

I

How frequently and how intensely we need that strength! A member of my church wrote me about it:

"I don't have problems with theology, though I like to hear interpretations and rattle my brains. I keep coming back to the thought that the big answer is *courage*. There are a lot of 'walking wounded' around. I think of all the big and little suffering and what we need, I think, is somehow to get the strength to face each day in spite of our inability to change our circumstances."

The "walking wounded" need strength: that's all of us at some time or other. I'm thinking not so much of the ebbing away of life's powers when death approaches, though there surely is that. I'm thinking more of those daily struggles to keep from going under

1

. . . the hurts, the anxieties, the slights, the runaway pressures, the unfair things, the incredible problems. And not only our own struggles but—almost more agonizing sometimes—the pains we know our friends are enduring. You could name them one by one.

Why? Why so much anguish? Ernie Pyle, that warm-hearted and winsome reporter of World War II Days, won a Pulitzer Prize for his work, but he sometimes gave in to the disillusionment of the world around him. Once he said, "I wish you would shine any of your light in my direction. God knows I've run out of light."[2] One day, centuries ago, the great writer, Dante, knocked at the gates of the Franciscan monastery in Luniguiana. A monk opened the door and asked, "What do you want?" Dante replied in one word, *"Peace!"*

The "walking wounded" need strength. In a small book of devotions called *Diary of Daily Prayer*, J. Barrie Shepherd asks for openness to "all whose way is tangled and obscure."[3] In the tangles and the obscurities of our daily struggles, again and again we sense the agonies of the walking wounded.

II

The Christian faith comes with the true and beautiful news that there is strength. For one thing, it is a strength that comes from *faith in the midst of realism.*

Faith knows the realism of our emotions. Back on the playground we learned that "big boys don't cry." Big girls, while they could get out the Kleenex now and then, weren't supposed to get angry or be very honest about their emotions, either. In the religious realm, questions were not really welcomed and we weren't supposed to admit to any doubts, especially in the presence of the preacher. When anything tragic happened we were supposed to keep a stiff upper lip because, "There, there, everything's going to be all right."

But sometimes things aren't all right, and big boys should cry! For the wounds are deep and the walking wounded can't find much strength unless they are helped to see that God knows, understands, and accepts the tear-stained face and the shout that asks, "Why?"

Our faith is faith that does not blink in the midst of the tough realities. Job, in spite of all that we have piously said about his patience, shook his fist at God: "Let the day perish wherein I was

2

born . . . I will not restrain my mouth. I will speak in the anguish of my spirit; I will complain in the bitterness of my soul."[4] Ah, yes, Job finally understood the majesty of a God who asked him, "Where were you when I laid the foundation of the earth?"[5] He moved on to a great affirmation of faith, "I know that thou canst do all things. . . . I had heard of thee by the hearing of the ear, but now my eye sees thee."[6] But Job came to that point only through the journey of realism.

B

Faith knows the realism of our emotions. It also lives within the realism of the Cross. During World War II, a Sunday School class was studying the crucifixion of Jesus. When the teacher told how Jesus died, one little boy leaped up in anger and cried out, "But where were the marines?"[7] He wanted a last-minute rescue. But no corps of marines, nor even any legion of angels, intervened. Had there been some Hollywood Happy Ending, we might thereafter have been able to find God in our triumphs and our successes. But we should not have been able to understand that we can also find God in our sufferings and defeats.

Christian faith understands the realism of the Cross. It endures Good Friday before it celebrates Easter. It knows that there is darkness as well as light. And it affirms that always there is God. One incisive writer put it,

> "If God could not speak to man in his grief, loneliness, and pain, he could not speak to man at all, for it is at these points that man's answers fade while his questions remain. The theoretical and speculative questions about why the misfortunes happen are never answered. God did not respond to agony with an argument. He responded with himself."[8]

We are reminded once more that the crucial question in life is not, "Why?" but "What now?" When we put that question to the problem of life's agonies, a part of the answer that comes sweeping back to us is, "Now you can take another step. Now you can go on." For even when your desolate question, "Why?" is answered only with silence, into that silence steals the Son of God himself. "God did not respond to agony with an argument. He responded with himself."

3

III

That leads us naturally to a further truth. The walking wounded find strength from a faith in the midst of realism. They find strength, also, from *faith in a Divinie companionship*.

More important than the burdens upon us, more crucial by far than the wounds with which we walk, is the Christ with whom we walk. He had been having a long conversation with His disciples. They all knew the end was near. This would probably be their last long talk. Jesus spoke in quiet tones about the comforting presence of the Spirit and about His confidence that, though He must die, they would see each other again. Then He said, "I have said this to you, that in me you may have peace. In the world you have tribulation; but be of good cheer, I have overcome the world."[9]

There's the realism: "In the world you have tribulation." And there's the promise of a Divine companionship: "In me you may have peace . . . I have overcome the world!"

The Apostle called Paul found the fulfillment of that promise. Paul—who was plagued with a disturbing illness that did not go away even when he prayed to God to remove it; Paul—who had first persecuted the Christians and then was persecuted far more for becoming one himself; this Paul—shares with us a serene and soaring confidence in a Divine companionship:

"... in all these things we are more than conquerors through him who loved us. For I am sure that neither death, nor life, nor angels, nor principalities, nor things present, nor things to come, nor powers, nor height, nor depth, nor anything else in all creation, will be able to separate us from the love of God in Christ Jesus our Lord."[10]

That is no philosophical answer to the whys and wherefores of suffering: it is confidence in a Divine companion.

William Hordern tells of visiting one day with a woman who was dying of cancer. In the midst of her pain, he said, she reflected a serenity and a triumphant faith in God's ultimate love. The next day, he sat in on a college seminar. The students were arguing that the suffering in the world made it impossible to believe in God.[11] They were wrestling with a philosophical question on an intellectual level. The cancer patient spoke from the depths of life and suffering

4

and approaching death. They were toying with glib solutions to puzzles. She was living and dying in faith—a faith which understood, at the only level that finally counts—that neither living or dying can separate us from God's Love. They had questions: she had a Companion. She knew a true and beautiful faith; that more important than the burdens upon us, more crucial by far than the wounds with which we walk, is the Companion with whom we walk.

During the Battle of Dunkirk, there came to a British port a handful of men led by their brigadier. An official received them and directed them to a rest center. "It's only a mile or two up the road," he said, speaking to the brigadier. Then, noticing the rank, he added, "Your men will find it easily. My chauffeur will be glad to run you up in my car." But the brigadier answered, "Thanks. But we've kept together through thick and thin, these lads and I, and I think we'll keep together to the end."

We have a God who keeps with us through thick and thin—and to the end. There is strength for the walking wounded, for

> ". . . though the wrong seems oft so strong,
> God is the ruler yet."[12]

References

1. Brophy, Don; *American Bread*; p. 51.
2. Quoted in Kennedy, Gerald; *A Second Reader's Notebook*; p. 145.
3. Shepherd, J. Barrie; *Diary of Daily Prayer*; p. 21.
4. Job 3:3; 7:11.
5. Job 38:4.
6. Job 42:2, 5.
7. Hordern, William and Otwell, John; *Proclamation: Lent*, p. 15.
8. Smith, Dana Prom; *An Old Creed for a New Day*; p. 62.
9. John 16:33.
10. Romans 8:37-39.
11. Hordern and Otwell; *op. cit.*; p. 16.
12. *The Methodist Hymnal*; No. 45; Stanza 3.

EXPLORING SOME FOUNDATIONS OF FAITH

God: From Whom All Blessings Flow

(Psalm 100; John 1:14-18)

A mountain climber slipped and found himself hanging on a single branch over a two thousand foot precipice. In frantic anxiety, he looked down and then he looked up. Searching the heavens, he cried, "Is there anybody up there who can help me?" To his astonishment, a thundering voice came back, "I'M HERE!" Trembling a little, he asked, "Who is it?" "GOD!" "What do you want me to do?" The voice thundered again, "LET GO!" The poor fellow remembered how far the bottom was below him and shakily asked, "What?" But the voice was even more insistent: "LET GO!" The climber looked down those two thousand feet once more, then back to the heavens, and called, "Is there anybody *else* up there?"

In the moment of his crisis, the poor fellow wasn't quite sure in what kind of God he could believe.

In our troubled times, it is important to us to know what the basics are. What are the foundations of faith? We have sometimes been told that the "world sets the agenda for the Church." It is indeed a biblical imperative that the world out there is the concern of the Church. What we are tempted to forget, however, is that the world may set the agenda for the Church, *but it does not set the message*. Dean William R. Inge once said that men who become wedded to the spirit of the times are likely to find themselves widowers in the next generation.[1] The Church has its own message, a gospel it has received. It brings that message to the world's agenda.

To keep that message straight, it is essential that we re-examine, from time to time, the foundations of our faith.

9

I

Begin by looking again at the "God from whom all blessings flow." President Pusey of Harvard said some years ago:

"It would seem to me that the finest fruit of serious learning should be the ability to speak the word *God* without reserve or embarrassment, certainly without adolescent resentment; rather with some sense of communion, with reverence and with joy."[2]

We need not spend time here arguing the pros and cons of the *existence* of God. We see Him sustaining the world around us. Joseph Addison wrote in 1712: "The Supreme Being has made the best argument for His own existence in the formation of the heavens and the earth . . . The word the heavens shout is God." A French infidel warned a peasant, "We will tear down your churches, burn your sacred books, destroy your pictures and demolish everything that reminds you of God!" The peasant answered simply but wisely, "You will leave us the stars, won't you?"[3]

God sustains the world around us, and we need not argue further for His existence. But even that fades to insignificance beside the greatest affirmation of all, that the day came when, "The Word became flesh and dwelt among us!" *"The Word,"* the Logos, that philosophical-theological term gathering up all that God has done and been, *became flesh*: here is the Fourth Gospel's announcement of the whole Christ-Event. Believing that, we shall not tarry to discuss further the *existence* of God.

II

Move, rather, to see and to say something about the Christian *understanding* of God. Do so by looking at the two halves of that concise and simple statement from the one-hundreth Psalm: "It is he that made us, and we are his."[4]

A

"It is He that made us." Here is the Christian understanding of the Creator-God. "I believe in God, the Father Almighty, maker of heaven and earth." "Praise God, *from whom all blessings* flow!" God has made us and all that is.

10

"*It is He that made us.*" That's an awesome statement. It ought to help us do away with what Deane William Fern has called, "The Abuse of God." God is abused when we make Him the god of the latest fad, whether it be the secular city or some wandering guru or the lord of fun and games. God is also abused when we force Him into the narrow molds of our own consciousness-raising or the rigidity of narrow beliefs.[5]

"*It is He that made us.*" The funeral of King Louis XIV of France was held in the magnificent Cathedral of Notre Dame, that place of towering greatness in Paris. Decorated with utmost lavishness, the Church was the scene of a distinguished gathering of nobility and royalty. The king's body was richly adorned, as if to remind everyone that death itself could not rob that royal form of its grandeur. Sophisticated persons from far and wide waited in awed silence for the great eulogy which the occasion demanded. What they heard, however, startled them to the depths of their noble hearts: "Only God is great!"

"*It is He that made us.*" God is greater than to be squeezed into our own little cookie cutters. A little boy, at the breakfast table, refused to eat his prunes. His exasperated mother shouted, "God won't like you if you don't eat your prunes! Go to your room!" He went, and a little later a terrible storm came up. The thunder and lightning was "something fierce." The mother began to think that her son might be afraid of the storm. She went up to his room. He was looking out the window, saying disgustedly, "What a fuss to make over a few prunes!"

He had hoped for something more from God. Had he been taught, "It is He that made us," he had a right to expect more.

"*It is He that made us.*" He is not limited by our stammering words. Goethe said one time, "The highest can never be spoken; it can only be acted." The Word became flesh and dwelt among us!

At this point we start, then: "*It is He that made us.*"

B

To the other half of the Psalmist's verse we confidently move: ". . . *and we are His.*"

God has made us. He has made all that is, anywhere. Yet we are His. Light travels six billion miles in a year. With our most sophisticated telescopes, we can see two billion light years in all direc-

11

tions. How many miles is that? If my feeble math is correct, it's 12 with 18 zeroes after it! And we know there are galaxies even beyond that. God made all that—*and cares for you*! "We are His!"

So He steadies our world when it begins to shake. He says through the Psalmist,

"When the earth totters, and all its inhabitants, it is I who keep steady its pillars."[6]

And again, in those words that inspired Martin Luther's "A Mighty Fortress":

"God is our refuge and strength, a very present help in trouble."[7]

Things may look shaky around here, but we are God's, and He steadies your world!

"*We are His.*" He is intensely, deeply involved in the sufferings of our world. Jurgen Moltmann, one of the most thoughtful theologians of our time, has put it in this striking way.

"The SS hanged two Jewish men and a youth in front of the whole camp. The men died quickly, but the death throes of the youth lasted for half an hour. 'Where is God? Where is He?' someone asked behind me. As the youth still hung in torment in the noose after a long time, I heard the man call again, 'Where is God now?' And I heard a voice in myself answer: 'Where is He? He is here. He is hanging on the gallows.' . . .

Any other answer would be blasphemy. There cannot be any other Christian answer to the question of this torment. To speak here of a God who could not suffer would make God a demon."[8]

When we suffer, He suffers with us.

"*We are His.*" We think of Fulton Oursler as a beautiful writer, a man of faith. There was a time in his life, however, when he hit the bottom. He was unemployed, his marriage was disintegrating, his health was breaking. He was an agnostic who hadn't been inside a Church for years. On a particularly dismal day, he was wandering down Fifth Avenue in New York. To his own amazement, he wandered into an open Church. There be began to pray. His prayer went like this:

"Lord, in ten minutes or less I may change my mind. I may scoff at this. Pay no attention to me then. For this little time I am in my right mind and heart. This is my best. Take it and forget the rest; and if you are really there, help me."[9]

Christian faith says God *is* really there. And He helps!

"*We are His*." Karl Marx' daughter once confessed to a friend that she had been raised without any religion and had never in fact felt very religious. She went on to say, however, "The other day I came across a beautiful little prayer which I very much wish could be true . . ." The friend asked, "What was the prayer? And Karl Marx' daughter began repeating, "Our Father, who art in heaven . . ."[10]

To which we say, "It is true! It's true! 'Our Father, who art in heaven . . .' It is He that made us, and we are His!"

References

1. Quoted in Ferm, Deane William; "The Abuse of God" in *Christian Century*; March 26, 1975; p. 308.

2. Pusey, Nathan M.; *The Age of the Scholar*; Cambridge, Mass.: Harvard University Press; 1965; p. 145.

3. Coniaris, Anthony M.; *Orthodoxy: A Creed for Today*; p. 62.

4. Psalm 100:3.

5. Ferm; *op. cit.*; pp. 308ff.

6. Psalm 75:3.

7. Psalm 46:1.

8. Moltmann, Jurgen; *The Crucified God*.

9. Oursler, Fulton; *Why I Know There Is A God*.

10. *Wholeness*; quoted in "New Pulpit Digest"; July-August, 1975, p. 33.

Christ: God in His Fulness and Man at His Highest

(Isaiah 40:1-5; John 1:1-5, 14; Philippians 2:5-10)

In Thornton Wilder's, *Our Town*, Dr. Gibbs has a talk with his son, George, about the lad's approaching marriage. Afterwards, frazzled, the doctor talks to his wife and says,

> "I tell you, Mrs. G., there's nothing so terrifying in the world as a son. The relation of a father to a son is the damndest, awkardest ------. I always come away feeling like a soggy sponge of hypocrisy."[1]

Have you ever reacted that way to your religion? You have a talk, as it were, with the Church—about its beliefs or its creeds—and you come away "feeling like a soggy sponge of hypocrisy."

We're trying to see if we can find a way to express a contemporary kind of faith in an up-to-the minute world, without getting soaked up in any soggy sponges. Searching for the foundations of our faith, we are compelled, surely, to ask, "*What do you see in Jesus?*" Can we answer that in some contemporary fashion? Helmut Thielicke, one of Europe's most incisive preachers, has been eminently concerned to state the faith in crisp, relevant terms. At the same time, he does not let his hearers run away from the fact that, ultimately, the Christian "must be led to face the granite greatness of a message that brooks no evasion," to the point where Jesus finally warns him, "Here you must leap or retreat."[2]

"What do you see in Jesus?" I am not going to turn to the stately cadences of the Apostles' Creed, nor to the theological intricacies of the Nicene Creed, for an answer. The fact that those affirmations have stood the test of time means that they have an inescapable validity. I invite you to see, however, if the "granite greatness" of the Christian's answer cannot be stated more concisely. I have tried to do so in these words,

"I believe in Jesus and affirm that in Him I see God in His fulness and man at his highest."

Break that into its two parts—God in His fulness, and man at his highest—and see if it is also a helpful way of stating your faith.

I

I believe in Jesus. In Him I see *God in His fulness.*

An exasperated lawyer was explaining a simple point of law to a client. He tried over and again, but he couldn't get through. Desparate, he finally jammed the law book into the man's hands and said, "Here. Read it for yourself!" After a minute, the attorney said impatiently, "Now do you get it?" And the answer was brief, "Sir, I can't read."

The opening assertion of the Fourth Gospel, as J. B. Phillips has worded it for us, is that, "In the beginning, God expressed himself." The more familiar statement is, "In the beginning was the Word." But, somehow, men couldn't "read" the word; they didn't get the point. And so, in the fulness of God's own time, He said it with piercing clarity. "God's Personal Expression became a human being!" That "personal expression" was Jesus of Nazareth. Sometimes our words, our expressions, *hide* our real selves. We talk fast and loud so no one will see us. And sometimes our words *unveil* our real selves. You don't have to be a psychiatrist to see that in some moments our words are "cover-ups" and on other occasions they are authentic revelations. There are biblical evidences that, at times, God purposely refused to let Himself be known. There came that day, however, when "the Expression of God became a human being"—written and announced for anyone with eyes to see and ears to hear. I am ready to affirm, therefore, that *in this man, we see God in His fulness.*

Bishop Robinson, in his perceptive book, *Honest To God,* tried to devastate any notion of a God "up there" who "came down" and became man. His point was well taken. In a space age, we do

15

well to avoid unnecessary confusion by using space images when we talk about God. It is also true, however, that the essential point in the traditional language about God "coming down" has nothing to do with *where* God is. The point is to deal with *who* God is. Even more, the point is to make this affirmation: *by an act of divine humility, God accepted for Himself the grubbiness and the glory of our existence.*

That act brought Charles Wesley to his feet singing,

> "O for a thousand tongues to sing
> My great Redeemer's praise,
> The glories of my God and King,
> The triumphs of His grace!"[3]

"In this man," he was saying, "*I see my God and King!*" Could he *prove* it? No, he could only *affirm* it. But can you "prove" the beauty of a sunset? Can you "prove" a man's yearning to be free? Can you "prove" a Rembrandt painting? Or a Beethoven symphony? Or the love in the eyes of a man and a woman, whether at their first anniversary or their fiftieth? Those things that count most deeply are not subject to "proof." But they may be true! *We live on the basis of our affirmations.*

With the Archbishop of Canterbury, then, I look to Jesus' birth in Bethlehem, to His forgiveness of sinners, to His washing His disciples' feet at the Last Supper, to His ghastly yet triumphant death outside Jerusalem . . . and I affirm that in that man there is the "depth of the divine humility."[4] I believe in Jesus and affirm that in Him I see God in His fulness.

II

More! I see *man at his highest.*

The granite greatness of the message that brooks no evasion surely includes this understanding, does it not? The hymn literally soars in its exultation,

> "All hail the power of Jesus' Name!
> Let angels prostrate fall;
> Bring forth the royal diadem
> And crown him Lord of all."[5]

To call Him "Lord of all" is to say something about His effect on our lives, for a lord is one who rules, who is in a position to control. The Christian allows Jesus to do that, because in Jesus he sees what he himself wants to be; he catches a vision of "himself at his highest." In a study group one time, some of us pondered several paintings of Christ, asking ourselves what the artist was saying about this man. We answered with words like, "Thoughtful . . . concerned . . . gentle . . . strong . . . compassionate . . . kind." I suspect that these were also words that we would like people to use if they were describing us. Here is a man who, *in fact*, was what we *would like to be*.

Paul was saying it, I think, as he wrote to the Christians in the city of Philippi.[6] Jesus, he declared, had always been God by nature, but He did not cling to His divinie prerogatives. He, by voluntary act, stripped Himself of privilege, and took the form of a servant. He humbled Himself and lived a life of utter obedience, even to the point of giving up His life. Paul, apparently, is implying that Jesus had existed from the beginning of time, but that is not the essential point. The crux of the matter is his description of Jesus' life on the tattered roads of Palestine, immersed in the lives of others. He shed the royal cloak of privilege and took on the burlap cloth of total obedience. Man at his highest!

Do you remember Arthur Miller's *Death of a Salesman*? I venture to predict that for a long time to come, people will turn back to the pathetic tale of Willy Loman if they want to understand what went wrong with the American character in the middle of the twentieth century. As his family stands around Willy's open grave, everyone tries to say something nice. Finally Biff blurts out the real truth: "He had the wrong dreams. All, all wrong." Happy is furious at this: "Don't say that!" But Biff goes on, for it is a long time since anyone in the Loman family has dared to speak the truth: "He never knew who he was."[7] In Jesus of Nazareth we are enabled to see who *we* really are. For there is man at his highest!

In the presence of our nation's noblest statue, the Lincoln Memorial in Washington, you cannot help but stand taller. If you have any sensitivity at all you are elevated in spirit. Reminded of that rough-hewn man's passion for human freedom and of his singular greatness, you come away a little more ready to put aside the lesser things and pursue the things that finally matter.

17

And in Jesus' presence? We stand a little taller! In Him we see expressed what is deepest in our lives. He has a purity and a selflessness and an unflinching courage that tug at our hearts. He lives close to His heavenly Father, but is never removed from the agonized needs of His fellow men. Are not these the qualities we would long to express? He, in His life and death and resurrection, is the person we want to be. Man at his highest!

After the Resurrection, Thomas demanded to see the nail prints in His Lord's hands. One writer disturbs us by reminding us,

"This is precisely what the world says to the Church. We who talk of walking the way of the Cross dare not show men our hands. For we have not been wounded for them, we have not suffered for them. We have done little more than preach for them."

We forever fail. But forever there is that vision of Man at his highest. Forever He calls us to stand tall and to be what we were meant to be.

References

1. Wilder, Thornton; *Our Town*; N.Y: Coward McCann, Inc.; 1938; p. 83.
2. Thielicke, Helmut, *I Believe: The Christian's Creed*; pp. xi, x.
3. *The Methodist Hymnal*, No. 1.
4. Ramsey, Archbishop Michael; *Image: Old and New*; Forward Movement Publications; p. 11.
5. *The Methodist Hymnal*, No. 72.
6. Philippians 2:5-10 (Phillips).
7. Miller, Arthur; *Death of a Salesman*; p. 138.
8. Kenrick, Bruce; *The New Humanity*; p. 90 (quoted in Walker, *ibid.*, p. 96).

Persons: Something Straight from God
(Genesis 1:26-31; 2:4b-7)

"I am just as human as you are," says Edith.

And Archie replies, "Oh yeah. . . . then prove you're just as human as me. Do something rotten."

So went a dialogue on the well-known TV program, "All in the Family," after Archie discovered that, for all these years, Edith had been *letting* him win their card games.

What does it mean to be human? To do "something rotten?" As we explore the foundations of our faith, it's not enough—it's essential, but it's not enough—to ask what we think of God or whether we love Jesus enough to follow Him. The life of faith has to go on to ask, "What does it mean to be human? A fully human person?"

Christian perspective sees persons as "something straight from God." The phrase is T. S. Eliot's:

> "Of course there's something in us
> In all of us which isn't just heredity,
> But something unique. Something we have been
> From eternity. Something . . . straight from God."[1]

That reaches, for its inspiration, all the way back to the opening chapter of Genesis; and brings its exploding truth right into the middle of your living room:

> "So God created man, in his own image, in the image of God he created him; male and female he created them . . . And God saw everything that he had made, and behold, it was very good."[2]

19

What kind of creature was this that He made? Maybe the more quaint version of the story tells us:

> ". . . a mist went up from the earth and watered the whole face of the ground—then the Lord God formed man of dust from the ground, and breathed into his nostrils the breath of life; and man became a living being."[3]

Take two phrases out of that, if you will, and you will begin to slice through to the center of the Christian understanding of man, this creature "straight from God." The two phrases? "Dust from the ground" and "the breath of life."

I

We are made out of "dust from the ground." See that first. We are limited . . . finite . . . earth-bound.

"Dust from the ground." Oh, not literally, of course. A little boy went to his mother and asked, "Is it true that from dust we have come and to dust we shall return?" "Yes," she replied. "Then there's somebody either coming or going under my bed!"

"Dust from the ground." Not literally, but a vivid way of reminding us of our crumminess. "Prove you're just as human as me. Do something rotten." Life is very specifically a gift from God. We "breathe His breath." We depend on Him. Our sin—our crumminess, our rottenness, our dustiness—is in our denial of that dependence. In that opening act of the biblical drama, the serpent teases Eve, taunting her to eat the forbidden fruit, saying: "You will not die. For God knows that when you eat of it your eyes will be opened, and you will be like God . . ."[4]

One wonders how much of human misery has been caused by persons, dust from the ground, who tried to be like God. Our concern for self-elevation, our "me-first" living, our wanting to be like God: is that the common denominator in war, in letting half the world go to bed hungry and cry itself to sleep, in family disruption, in so many fractured dreams?

We are made from dust of the ground. In Christian terms, we are sinners. We do that which we ought not to do, and leave undone the things that need doing. How much we need to be set free! On one of the more intense days of His life, Jesus goes to the side of

Mary and Martha. Their brother, and His good friend, Lazarus, has died. But Jesus walks out to the tomb, and there He calls with a loud voice, "Lazarus, come forth!" The dead man does come out, his hands and feet bound with bandages and his face wrapped with a cloth, in the ancient manner of burial. To those near him, Jesus says, "Unbind him and let him go!"[5]

Whatever the shackles of our dust-covered lives—the chains of inferiority or guilt or regret or depression or alcoholism, or the thousand hand-cuffs we have locked on ourselves by our own sin— Jesus' word is, "My friend, come forth!" And to those awful, gripping shackles: "Unbind him, and let him go!"

Jesus sees in each of us the "something straight from God" and He knows that there is more there than just "dust from the ground." He calls us on to that "something more."

II

What that means is caught up for us in that other phrase from Genesis. We are not only "dust from the ground." *but we have "the breath of life."* Move to that now:

". . . the Lord God formed man of dust from the ground, *and breathed into his nostrils the breath of life; and man be- came a living being."*

Hugh Prather in his little book, *I Touch the Earth, the Earth Touches Me*, talks about the problem of not being "phony," and then he asks a disturbing question: "I guess it could be said that I'm being 'genuine,' but genuinely what?"[6] Prather may be confused, but the Christian faith says that a genuinely authentic human person is one who has received "the breath of life." He knows that he never quite leaves the fact that he is "dust from the ground" but he also knows that he has been invigorated by the breath of God Himself. That intense and beautiful hymn rightly has us pray,

"Breathe on me, breath of God,
Till I am wholly thine,
Till all this earthly part of me
Glows with thy fire divine."[7]

"The breath of life . . . a living being!" What does that mean?

It means that our crumminess, our dustiness, is not all there is. One day in 1903, a bishop of the United Brethren Church in Dayton, Ohio, made a firm statement that he thought settled things. He said, "God did not intend for men to fly around the sky like a bird, for if he had intended it he would have given men wings like the birds." On the seventeenth of December in that same year, two sons of that bishop, Orville and Wilbur Wright, made the first flight in a machine heavier than air. They ushered in a whole new age. Now, with all our concerns about jet noises and air pollution, maybe the good bishop was right! But in another sense, surely we say this: that God intended, always, for men and women to soar to new heights of loving, new levels of service, new horizons of commitment.

To those new heights, Jesus always calls us. When we would grovel in our awareness of the dust from the ground that holds us down, He would remind us that we have been unbound and let loose. We are meant to be "living beings."

Part of what it means to live on those heights is to touch the lives of other persons. Malcolm Muggeridge, the English journalist and broadcaster, was in contact with Mother Teresa in Calcutta. He was to do a television interview with the humble nun who had totally immersed herself in the lives of the desperately poor, the starving and the dying, of that city. When all the technical arrangements had been completed, Mother Teresa wrote to Muggeridge and said, "Now let us do something beautiful for God." For her, that's what life is all about: to "do something beautiful for God." Simply and straightforwardly, that means, as far as she is concerned, to help some poor person die within sight of a loving face. The way to do something beautiful for God is to be in touch with people.

For you: I can't tell you who or where those people are, or how to do it. I can only say, "Open your life to the love of God. Let Him breathe the breath of life deeply into your soul. Then follow your heart."

Albert Camus says somewhere,

> "Don't walk in front of me
> I may not follow.
> Don't walk behind me
> I may not lead.
> Walk beside me
> And just be my friend."

It may be that for you to "breathe the breath of God" means simply—yet not so simply—to walk with empathy beside someone. Sympathy means to feel sorry for someone. Empathy is a richer term. It means to "feel with" someone. It is to feel, "Your hurt is in my heart, your loss is in my prayers, your sorrow is in my soul, and your tears are in my eyes."

In the play *The Rainmaker*, Lizzie, the daughter tells a friend about her father:

"Some nights I'm in the kitchen washing the dishes. And Pop's playing poker with the boys. Well, I'll watch him real close. And at first I'll just see an ordinary middle-aged man— not very interesting to look at. And then, minute by minute, I'll see little things I never saw in him before. Good things and bad things—queer little habits I never noticed he had— and ways of talking I never paid any mind to. And suddenly I know who he is—and I love him so much I could cry! I want to thank God I took the time to see him real."[8]

To see and to be "real" is to go way beyond the dingbat level of doing "something rotten." It is to know that, while you are "dust from the ground," you are also far more. It is to know that the Divine Creator has breathed into you the breath of life. And that the Master Himself calls to you, saying, "Come forth!"

You're meant to be alive! You're "something straight from God!"

References

1. Quoted; "New Pulpit Digest"; May-June 1975; p. 69.
2. Genesis 1:27, 31.
3. Genesis 2:6-7.
4. Genesis 3:4-5.
5. John 11:43-44.
6. Prather, Hugh; *I Touch the Earth, the Earth Touches Me*; pages not numbered.
7. *The Methodist Hymnal*; No. 133; Stanza 3.
8. Nash, N. Richard; *The Rainmaker* (NY: Grosset and Dunlap; Bantam Books, 1957); Act 3; p. 102.

23

The Church: A People on the March

(Ezekiel 37:1-6; Matthew 22:34-40)

"Can these bones live?" Ezekiel was a spooky sort of fellow. He was always seeing some kind of vision. One day he saw a valley filled with bones. They were dry. They were a symbol of the whole nation of Israel—a scattered, brittle, unfaithful people. The penetrating question was, "Can these bones live?"

We look at a so-called "second Israel," the Church. Some days we ask the same question, "Can these bones live? These very dry, very brittle bones? Can they come alive?" Walt Kelly's Pogo said something one day that also zeroes in on the Church: "We have faults which we have hardly used yet."

Ezekiel found hope, however. God told him,

"Say to the bones: Hear the word of the Lord, and I will cause breath to enter you, and you will live. . . . I will put my Spirit within you, and you shall live."[1]

Hope, for Israel, was to be in response to the Spirit of God. So, also, for the second Israel! Hope for the Church is not in one more gimmick, not in the mindless embracing of every flea-brained idea the world throws at us, but in our listening to a voice that calls, *"O dry bones, hear the word of the Lord."*

The bones called the Church are already stirring with some signs of vitality, of course. Martin Marty, in a perceptive bicentennial essay, reflected on Pogo's words. Then this astute church historian said of the Churches, "They have *virtues* they haven't even used yet

24

. . . In thousands of local situations, religious people are putting their faith to work."[2]

As we continue our re-examination of the foundations of faith, I invite you now to look at the Church.

Can these bones live? With "faults we haven't even used yet," can we "hear the word of the Lord" and respond to His Spirit? I want to suggest that if these bones do live, we will be *a people on the march*.

Nestor Paz was a young Bolivian University student. He gave his life in a guerilla campaign to improve the situation of his people. We would not have agreed with his philosophy but in a letter home he said something that can speak to the Church. He wrote,

"Yesterday I read a little of the Apostles, their first steps, their hesitations, their discoveries, their cowardice, their confidence in the 'triumph.' It gave me new courage and strengthened my desire to be in the vanguard, to be a prophet of a people on the march."[3]

A people on the march have at least four qualities. They also say something about the Church.

I

First, this simple quality; a people on the march *rehearse*. Sometimes on a fall afternoon when my office windows are open, I can hear the quiet roll of drums. The High School band is out getting ready to march at the football games. They rehearse before they perform.

For the community called the Church, our rehearsal is in the sanctuary. When the United Methodist Council of Bishops met in Minneapolis in 1975, the theme of the morning worship one day was, "The Priority of Praise." It was an incisive reminder that we belong in the sanctuary before we belong in the class room, the committee room, or on the streets. Doxology—the praise of God from whom all blessings flow—comes before budget or education or social concern or missions or any other program in the life of the Church. We belong in the sanctuary first.

II

Move quickly to a second quality of a people on the march: *they know who the drummer is.* If half a dozen drums each beat a different rhythm, the band had better know to whom it is listening, or there will be hopeless confusion in the ranks.

A people on the march know who the drummer is. Lots of drums are calling for our attention as Christians. They have an appealing beat, those drums of drink and drugs, of complacency and convenience, of fundamentalism and free-wheeling. *An appealing beat! But the drummer for the Church is Jesus Christ!* Was it not Thoreau who made the incisive observation that if the Christian seems out of step with the world it is because he hears the beat of another drum? It's a revolutionized, tumultuous world in which we live. Moral tumult, economic tumult, political tumult, religious tumult: how easy it is to lose our bearings! The noises of the world pound at our ears!

But the Church listens for the incessant drum beat of its Master, "Jesus Christ . . . the same yesterday, today, and forever."[4] One writer calls Him "the still point of the turning world." The Apostle Paul calls us ". . . to mature manhood, to the measure of the stature of the fullness of Christ; so that we may no longer be children, tossed to and fro and carried about with every wind of doctrine . . ."[5]

Like the big, bad wolf huffing and puffing at the houses of the three little pigs, all sorts of wild ideas keep trying to blow the Church down and toss us all around. They will succeed unless we know to whom we belong. We'll blow away in all directions unless we know where we're going because we know who the drummer is.

III

See a third quality of a people on the march: *they work together.* You know that a band on the field with crooked lines hasn't worked together very well. And it wouldn't be much of a band if a lot of guys and gals with instruments just walked around, helter-skelter. A people on the march move together.

So also the Church. If those bones are to live and to move, they will come alive together, march together. I watched open heart surgery once. I still remember the incredible work of the surgeon who stood in one place and worked with unrelieved intensity for six hours. Equally impressive, though, was the fact that there were as many as twenty other people in the operating room, each with a job to do, working with faultless precision. Not the surgeon alone, but a whole team of workers was required. The effective life of the Church also takes a whole team of workers.

A football team was being badly beaten. The coach began to shout instructions from the sidelines. "Give the ball to Caldwell." Caldwell got the ball and was thrown for a five yard loss. Again the coach yelled, "Give the ball to Caldwell." Caldwell tried the middle of the line and lost ten yards. Undaunted, the coach called again, "Give the ball to Caldwell!" This time, Caldwell tried to pass but was sacked by the whole defensive line. Now the quarterback called time out, came to the sidelines, and said "Caldwell don't want the ball!" The effective life of the Church requires that many "carry the ball."

Paul says that in the Church God has appointed apostles, prophets, teachers, helpers, administrators.[6] And if he were writing in our time: Commission members, lay leaders, trustees, officers. And all are necessary. Each, in his or her own way, has an essential gift to bring. The one thing I don't hear Paul asking for is people whose "gift" is *folded arms*. You know: the temptation to see a problem, fold our arms, and say, "What are *you* going to do about it?" David MacLennan once challenged his people this way:

". . . make the Church what you know it ought to become, can become, too, since Christ loved it and gave His life for it. At the end of the day, God will not ask you what kind of a Church you belonged to, but what kind of a Church you longed for. Longed for enough—that is—to pray for, witness within, and strive for."[7]

A people on the march work together.

IV

Still a fourth quality describes such a people: *they move outside*. They rehearse, they know who the drummer is, they work together, and then they have to move outside. You can't stay indoors with a marching band! You have to go march for somebody!

So also the Church. It gathers to enrich its life; it scatters to serve the world or it isn't much of a Church. A little girl who lived in a very big house went to visit her young friend who lived in an apartment. She had never been in that kind of a building before. She was startled the first time she heard voices and music from the next apartment. Her hostess said proudly, "At our house, we have neighbors just through the wall." God made a world like that: neighbors just through the wall . . . and in the next Church pew . . . and next door . . . in the next block . . . in the next nation . . . and all over!

Worship and education and committee meetings and all the rest, then, are not enough. We have to move outside! In the kind of truth to be found in overstatement, the prophet Amos has God look at the people and their worship and say, "I hate, I despise your feasts, and I take no delight in your solemn assemblies." Amos' people thought they were awaiting "the day of the Lord" and did not need to serve "the people of the Lord." So he had to thunder them right out of their solemn sanctuaries:

> "Seek good, and not evil,
>   that you may live . . .
> . . . let justice roll down like waters,
>   and righteousness like an everflowing stream."[8]

And if that does not cascade over all the ramparts of our defensiveness, here is Jesus Himself blowing away forever the distinction between sanctuary and street: "You shall love the Lord your God with all your heart, and with all your soul, and with all your mind. This is the great and first commandment. *And a second is like it*: You shall love your neighbor as yourself."[9]

We've heard that so often it sounds trite, but it's really an explosion of dynamite, clearing a path for a whole way of life. To be in the sanctuary, praising the Lord your God: that's absolutely essential. But also and equally: you shall love your neighbor as yourself. "To worship rightly," says John Greenleaf Whittier, "is to love each other. . . . Each smile a hymn, each kindly deed a prayer."[10] Alexander Solzhenitsyn has one of his characters in prison say: "It is not our level or prosperity that makes for happiness but the kinship of heart to heart and the way we look at the world."[11] The Church looks at the world with the conviction that it is crucial that there be a community of people who build the "kinship of heart to heart." From the strength of that kinship the Church relates to the world, seeking to touch its fever with the cooling hand of love and —strangely enough—to thaw its coldness with the warm embrace of love.

A people on the march moves outside. The Church always moves to the world. Some years ago in England, the king was on the radio. In the middle of his speech, an electrical wire broke, preventing his voice from being carried to those who were listening. Realizing that there was no time to fix anything, an alert workman in the studio took the two wire ends in his hands, and became himself a part of the circuit, allowing the King's speech to continue.

Through the workman, the King's work was done. Someone observed, "We are gap closers in the workshop of the Almighty." It may still be that you and I can help close the gap between the Church with all its faults and the Church God needs in our time and place.

And the dry bones, having heard the word of the Lord, will come alive!

References

1. Ezekiel 37:5, 14.
2. *Time*; October 27, 1975; p. 84.
3. Paz, Nestor; *My Life for My Friends*; p. 65.
4. Hebrews 13:8.
5. Ephesians 4:13-14.
6. I Corinthians 12:28.
7. MacLennan, David A.; *Joyous Adventure*; p. 137.
8. Amos 5:14, 24.
9. Matthew 22:37-39.
10. *The Methodist Hymnal*, No. 199, Stanza 1.
11. Solzhenitsyn, Alexander; *Cancer Ward*; (NY: Grosset & Dunlap, Bantam Books, 1969); p. 266.

The Bible: The Book One Always Comes Back To

(II Timothy 3:14-17)

As Henry Drummond lay dying, he called a close friend to his side. He asked him to read from the Bible. When the friend finished, Drummond said quietly, "That is the book one always comes back to."[1] John Wesley, an avid reader who read nearly every worthwhile book published in his lifetime, nevertheless said one time, "I am a man of one book—the Bible."[2]

My mother died while I was still too young really to remember her. But I have her Bible, and that tells me a lot about her. She must have come back to it time and time again, for the cover is rubbed thin, the pages smudged, and many of the great passages are underlined.

It's a book one always comes back to when he or she is concerned about the foundations of faith. Here we find the undergirding of all that we say about God, about Jesus, about persons, about the Church.

We won't come back to it, of course, as a kind of spiritual magic. Some people think they can put blindfolds on and be helped by pointing to some magic passage. They might, of course, be lucky enough to land on Jesus' reassuring promise, "Lo, I am with you always." They might also, however, have the luck of the proverbial guy who struck two passages in a row: "Judas went out and hanged himself" and "Go thou and do likewise." The Bible isn't spiritual magic.

Nor will we come back to it as if science had taught us nothing in four thousand years. The world was *not* created in six days. Science has taught us otherwise, but that doesn't touch the central conviction of the Genesis writer, namely, that God is the source of it all.

And we won't come back to the Bible with our literary and logical discrimination hiding in the corner. There's a difference, after all, as any high school sophomore can tell you, between prose and poetry, between history and fond imagination. Even in the Bible, not every written sentence can possibly be taken literally: Jesus would not have wanted you to cut off your hand or poke your eye out, although you can find Him quoted as advising both of those things.[3]

We won't come back to the Bible as if it could not stand analysis. A man who was interested in old books ran into a friend who had just thrown away an old Bible he found in his attic. The friend happened to mention that "somebody named Guten-something-or-other" had printed it. "Not Gutenberg!" gasped the book lover. "You idiot! That was one of the first books ever printed. A copy sold at auction for more than $400,000!" "Well," said the other fellow, "mine wouldn't have been worth anything. Some guy named Martin Luther had scribbled all over it." Your Bible will stand up to your scribbling all over it. It's devotional. It's inspirational. It's also greatly worth your consistent study, writing in its margins and between its lines, jotting down your new insights and asking your tough questions.

It's a book we always come back to. As Paul says to Timothy, it is "inspired by God and profitable for teaching, for reproof, for correction, and for training in righteousness . . ."[4] In 1540, Bishop Bonner placed six copies of it in St. Paul's Cathedral in London, and people formed great lines in order to have a few minutes to read it for themselves. We don't do that. Sometimes we even ignore it. But if we are concerned about the foundations of our faith, we will come back to it again and again for at least three reasons: to see God more clearly, to see ourselves more clearly, and to see life more clearly.

I

First: see God more clearly.
Late one night, a Hindu came to the bungalow of a missionary.

31

"My son is very ill," he explained. "We have carried him long miles to you." The missionary immediately started to get the lad to a hospital. "Wait!" said the Hindu. "First I want you to read from your sacred book and pray." The puzzled missionary replied, "But you are a Hindu. You have over 3,000 gods. Why do you ask me to read from the Bible?" "Because your Christ understands better, and the words from that Book sound like words from the heart of God."

It's a book we come back to when we would see more clearly the heart of God. In the nineteenth century, the poet-philosopher Swinburne re-wrote the Christmas message. He cried out,

> "Glory to man in the highest,
> For man is the master of things."

But the Bible reminds us always that *God* is the master of things. If we would recall only His sternness and His justice, Scripture brings us up short and floods us with the awareness that "there's a wideness in God's mercy, like the wideness of the sea." But if we would remember only His forgiveness and His love, we are again stopped in our tracks and asked to walk with Him "in lowly paths of service." He is, in Hosea's word, "the Holy One" but He is also "in our midst."[5] With the triumphant anthem in the Book of Revelation we sing,

> "Worthy art thou, our Lord and God,
> to receive glory and honor and power. . . ."[6]

but we also affirm, with the Fourth Gospel, that this God "became flesh and dwelt among us."[7]

The Bible is the book we always come back to if we would see God more clearly.

II

Second: we see ourselves more clearly.
Have you heard the old ditty?

> The photographer got ready,
> He rearranged my head.
> 'Do you want a pretty picture,
> Or a likeness?' then he said.

The Bible gives us a likeness of ourselves. It's not always a pretty picture. We look a lot like Adam and Eve. Some people think of them as an actual couple in history. Some think of them as representatives of all people in all history. No matter, really, for in either case they look like us and we look like them. They had Paradise, but because of their own selfish concerns they tossed it out the garden gate. Or, rather, that's where they got tossed. It's a pretty clear picture of our human sin and personal folly. The Church's great Prayer of General Confession has us pray, "We have erred and strayed from Thy ways like lost sheep."

But God does not give up. No matter what, it is still true that "it is He who has made us, and we are His."[8] There is a second Adam, Christ. And we look like Him, too. Where sin abounds, grace much more abounds. Those who are in Christ are new creations.[9]

Have you ever looked into a discolored mirror? Or tried to use a tin can as a mirror? You can't see yourself clearly. You can't see to comb your hair very well. Paul, in another connection, said, "Now I see through a glass darkly."[10] Left to ourselves, we get a distorted image. We think of ourselves more highly than we ought to think . . . or we get unrealistically down on ourselves. The Bible brings the picture into clear focus: sinners, yes; like Adam, yes . . . but forgiven sinners, set everlastingly free by the love of the second Adam, Jesus Christ!

We come back to the Bible and we see ourselves more clearly.

III

Then, this, third: we see life more clearly. That is, we see the exciting intermingling of challenge, comfort, and joy.

There's challenge. Two little girls were having a heated discussion about the name of the last book of the Bible. Finally one, totally exasperated, shouted, "I tell you, the Bible does not end with Timothy! It ends with Revolutions!" She was confused about the Book of Revelation, but she spoke a deeper truth than she knew. The Bible is permeated with revolutions in its ideas about the way we live. It comes with challenge. "Love the Lord your God . . . and your neighbor as yourself." That's not easy. "Love your enemies and pray for those who persecute you." That's not easy. "Do not lay up for yourselves treasures on earth . . . but treasures in heaven." That's not easy. "Seek first God's kingdom and His righteousness." That's not easy.

There's challenge and lots of it.

But there's comfort, too. It was late on a very dark evening. I was at a camp, making my way from the lodge to my cabin. The path was unfamiliar and I soon wandered off it. I tripped over a stump, got up and walked into a bush. A flashlight would have solved all my problems. Life is like that sometimes: the path is rough and full of things over which we stumble. The way is dark. In the midst of it all, the Bible can help us to see the way. The Psalmist says, "Thy word is a lamp to my feet, and a light to my path."[11] With that light we won't see all the answers, but we may at least see a sign on the pathway: "Peace I leave with you; my peace I give to you . . . Neither death, nor life, nor angels, nor principalities, nor things present, nor things to come, nor powers, nor height, nor depth, nor anything else in all creation will be able to separate us from the love of God in Christ Jesus our Lord."[12]

Woven in among the challenge and the comfort, there is joy. Helen Keller was one of the miracles of our times. Deaf, dumb, and blind, she might have travelled over the whole highway of life, pitying herself. At best, she might have found nothing more in the Bible than help for her own trouble. Instead, listen to what she says: "The lightness with which people often utter the word Bible and dismiss it as a book for sick souls always amazes me. It seems to me it is the most-read volume on earth because it sanctions happiness . . ." We need, she says, to learn to ". . . form the habit of going to the Bible in bright moments as well as in trouble . . ."[13]

This book we always come back to enables us to see life more clearly, to glimpse the intermingling of challenge, and comfort, and the wellsprings of deepest joy. The word of the Christmas angel is a word for all of life: "I bring you glorious news of great joy which is for every person!"

Again and again go back to be sustained by that. And your faith will find again its solid foundations.

References

1. Quoted; Miller, Donald; *Fire In Thy Mouth*; p. 85.
2. Quoted; "Pulpit Digest"; January 1962; p. 15.

34

3. Matthew 5:29–30.
4. II Timothy 3:16.
5. Hosea 11:9.
6. Revelation 4:11.
7. John 1:14.
8. Psalm 100:3.
9. II Corinthians 5:17.
10. I Corinthians 13:12.
11. Psalm, 119:105.
12. John 14:27; Romans 8:38–39.
13. American Bible Society pamphlet for Universal Bible Sunday, 1960, "The Book for Everyone," p. 6.

Let Us Pray

With distressed thoughts and troubled minds, we turn to You, O God of serenity and calm. So much keeps churning inside us: We wonder if we will ever be able to settle down. Then we recall that there was One who said to the raging waters, "Peace! Be still!" With quivering but audacious faith, we claim those words for our own. We remember that beyond the uncertain tumult of our days there is the steady march of the centuries. We yield our smallness to a grandeur beyond our faint imagining. We are still . . . and know that Thou art God!

Amen!

EXPLORING SOME HARD QUESTIONS OF FAITH

Take It To the Lord in Prayer
Does prayer do any good?
Mark 1:35; Matthew 26:36–46; Matthew 7:7–8; James 5:15

It is good for us to wrestle with the hard questions of faith. For in the wrestling, we grow. If we never do any doubting or questioning, (a) we come off as opinionated, and (b) we're probably dishonest. Miguel de Unamuno put it, "Faith which does not doubt is dead faith."[1]

I once asked the congregation of which I am pastor to tell me their tough questions. I gave them a questionnaire. It was a hazardous thing to do! The ushers handed them to me and sighed, "We know what you're going to be preaching about for the next five years!" We're full of questions!

For example, there is the question, or rather, there are the myriad questions, which we ask about prayer. One of the earliest notes in Jesus' ministry, after an exhausting day of preaching, recruiting disciples, teaching, and healing is that, ". . . in the morning, a great while before day, he rose and went out to a lonely place, and there he prayed."[2] One of the final notes, as life's last shadows were closing in around Him, is that He went to a secluded garden and ". . . fell on his face and prayed."[3] In between, He said, "Ask, and it will be given you. . . ."[4] The Epistle of James says, "The prayer of a righteous man has great power in its effects."[5] And one of our favorite hymns gathers up our sin and grief, our troubles and discouragements, our weakness and our burdened cares and invites us, "Take it to the Lord in prayer!"[6]

Still we ask a ton of hard questions! About intercession, about whether God hears, about keeping our faith when we don't get the

39

answers we want, about why God needs us to tell Him what to do, about why we bow our heads instead of looking up. Take it to the Lord in prayer—but the questions keep coming, and I think we can boil them down to this one: *Does prayer do any good*? I want to try to respond in two ways: first, by clearing away some road-blocks that have bothered us, and second, by turning on to some freeways that can help us.

I

Some roadblocks have hindered us in the life of prayer. Let's see if we can set them aside.

A

One roadblock has been too limited a notion of prayer. We have confined prayer to specified times and places and have felt guilty when we missed them. I must confess to you that I do not always pray at a regular time, morning and evening. That's a confession, not a boast, for I think most of us would benefit from a more disciplined schedule, but I must also say that I think a day does not go by but what I pray . . . maybe in the car, maybe while walking, maybe while waiting for some habitually tardy friend. And maybe with just a word: "Thanks!" Or, "Help!" Or, "God!" We have had too restricted an idea of the language to use in prayer. We have felt frustrated when we couldn't master "Thee" and "Thou," let alone "dost" and "wilt" and "art." And so we have not prayed at all. But God surely is not blocked by our language. In a delightful book I read recently, the five-year-old who is the central figure just starts right in with, "Mister God, it's Anna!" J. Barrie Shepherd went to Edinburgh to study about prayer. He came away saying, "I learned that prayer is not greatly concerned with words; it is a matter of life lived in the presence of the Lord."[7] We may set aside the roadblock which limits our notion of prayer to particular times, places, or words.

B

Another roadblock has been the confusion of prayer with meditation. For a long time, there have been those who have said prayer is nothing but a kind of meditative self-hypnosis, a time to think clearly. Now, I'm all in favor of clear thinking, and engaging in what psychology calls auto-suggestion may well be helpful, but it is not prayer. Nor, in terms of the more recent fads, is "relaxation response" or "transcendental meditation" prayer. The essential difference is this: meditation is done with one eye on yourself, maybe with one eye on the blood-pressure machine. As one who has to watch blood-pressure, I don't downgrade that. But it is not prayer. Meditation, at least as it has been popularly understood in our time, funnels in on one's self. Prayer expands away from self to God and other people. Set aside another roadblock by clearing up the confusion between prayer and meditation.

C

One more roadblock has been our inadequate expectations about how prayer might be answered. Sometimes, for reasons we may or may not understand, the answer has to be, "No." A parent has to say that to a child sometimes, and God has to say it to us. Jesus said, "Ask . . . seek . . . knock,"[8] but He does not teach that every wish will be granted. He went into Gethsemane praying that the Cup of pain and death could be taken away, and came out knowing that there was no way but the Cross. A poet said it this way:

> "I have shouted into the silence
> but have heard only the echo of my own cries.
> God, why don't you answer?
>
> My child, sometimes I answer,
>   but you can't hear me over the hi-fi.
> Sometimes I answer and you misinterpret.
>   But I'm not giving up—
> even though you've just hung up again."[9]

Set aside the roadblock that limits the way prayer might be answered.

II

Turn, then, from roadblocks that bother to *freeways that can help us.*

A

There is, for example, the freeway of confession. Prayer, surely, begins with adoration and praise, with thanks to the God who has given all good things. But it quickly moves to confession. We've thought of that as negative, as being one of the roadblocks. Instead, it can be a freeway . . . a time and a way in which we ask God to help us set aside the weights, the burdens, the wrongs, the sins that have held us down and blocked us from responding to His good gifts. A three-year-old girl found her two-year-old brother sitting and splashing in the middle of a mud puddle. He was a mess. His sister was indignant with him but he ignored her. Finally, summoning up all the authority she could think of, she said to him firmly, "Go tell Mommy she wants you!"[10] Our confession, our "Lord, have mercy upon us," is our telling God He wants us and we're in need of a bath and some clean clothes. We hear His cleansing word, "My child, you are forgiven!", and confession becomes a freeway to new life.

B

There's another kind of freeway in our prayer life. We call it intercession. It is praying for others. That seems unreal to some people. They understand that some good things may happen to themselves when they pray, but they cannot fathom how their praying could affect another person. I have to say in response that, for me, there is nothing more natural than going to the One who cares for each person everywhere as if there were no other and saying, "Father, I'm so concerned about . . . ." and then naming names in his presence. Having prayed for myself, how can I stop there? Intercession is not a substitute for the actions I ought to take on behalf of those persons. It is not a way of coercing God to do what the conditions of a law-abiding universe will not allow. Intercession, rather, is trying to clear the channels for the widest possible divine-human cooperation. Years ago, George Harkness put it this way:

> "What happens in intercessory prayer cannot be fully explained and scientifically demonstrated. Its validity is, and probably always will be, a matter of faith and experience rather than proof. However, if one accepts the basic assumption that God is real and that there are spiritual forces in the

universe which transcend though they do not violate natural law, the way is open to (the possibility of intercession.)"[11]

Intercession—your concern for others in the presence of your Heavenly Father—can become an open freeway in the life of prayer.

C

Another freeway can be the spirit of commitment. It's the movement away from telling God anything—and listening to what He has to say to us. In her recent book, Avery Brooke says that all prayer "has one effort in common: to take us out of the ruts in which our insights have been exhausting themselves."[12] Archbishop William Temple used to say that the proper theme for a Christian prayer is not, "Please do for me what I want," but "Please do with me what You want." That's to let God lift us out of our ruts. That's commitment. It can be an exciting freeway.

And so we ask again, "Does prayer do any good?" A three-year-old boy was playing doctor to his four-year-old sister's doll. After a rigorous examination of the doll, he turned to his sister and said, "Your child will not get well, lady." She answered, "You are a no-good doctor. I'll get me another one." "You can't," he replied, "because there isn't another one." "Then I'll tell God to make her well!" "O.K., lady, but you don't *tell* God; you *ask* Him."

When we have done our asking—then what? Then we proceed with both assurance and caution. Assurance, because hosts of people, for example, have prayed for the recovery of loved ones and have seen the tide turn and flow upward in ways no doctor could explain and they have claimed the victory of prayer. We praise God with them. Caution, because others have been prayed for with equal earnestness and depth of faith and they have died. In life's many and varied difficult circumstances, some have prayed for courage to go on and have found it with radiant beauty, while others of equal devotion have sagged and found life all but unbearable.

Does prayer do any good then? Does it work? Lacking divine wisdom, we will not presume to dictate the conclusions. But this much we know: in prayer we join hands with the God who is both Creator and Father. By His power, we discover that, whatever the conclusion, there is a victory . . . the victory of life in His loving presence.

43

In Our Lady's Church in the city of Copenhagen, there is a statue of our Lord, done by the sculptor, Thorwaldsen. It is a striking statue from any angle, but its unique feature is this: you cannot see Christ's face except when you are kneeling and looking up. To live as those who see the face of Christ: that is prayer.

References

1. Quoted, *Christian Century*; March 3, 1976; p. 189.
2. Mark 1:35.
3. Matthew 26:39.
4. Matthew 7:7.
5. James 5:16.
6. *The Methodist Hymnal*, No. 261.
7. Shepherd, J. Barrie; *Diary of Daily Prayer*, p. 6.
8. Matthew 7:7-8.
9. Hale, Robert; in *Alive Now!*; November-December 1974; p. 29.
10. *The Upper Room*; July-August 1975.
11. Harkness, Georgia; *Prayer and the Common Life*; p. 79.
12. Quoted, *Christian Century*; op. cit.; p. 201.

Everest and Chimborazo
What do I do when I don't succeed?

Philippians 4:8–13

The various stories of the conquests and near-conquests of Mt. Everest hold an unceasing fascination. In 1953, as a coronation gift to Elizabeth II, Hillary and Tensing announced that they had inched their way to that great peak 29,002 feet above sea level. In one breathless moment they had finally seen the other side of the mountain: this was the peak of Everest! They stood together on top of the world!

Now along comes the Smithsonian Institution saying they only get second prize. Everest is Number Two. Number One—the highest spot in the world—belongs (on recalculation) to Mt. Chimborazo in Ecuador.

Isn't it always the way? Just when you think you've reached the summit, climbed your own personal Mt. Everest of achievement, some clown waves down at you from *his* Mt. Chimborazo! You hardly finish talking about your fish before this clod over here tells you about a bigger one. You don't even finish your sentence about the most marvelous grandchild in the world before the next woman has whipped all those cute pictures out of her purse. You finally squeak out opening count in the bridge game and someone makes a pre-emptive bid. By an incredible feat of scrimping and cutting corners, you manage at long last to put $100 in the bank, and someone making less than you are talks about his last conversation with his broker! Just when you make your breathless way to Everest, someone calmly waves at you from Chimborazo.

It's one of the hard questions that tests our faith: What do I do when I don't succeed? But life cannot always be lived on Chimborazo. Nor should it be. The pounding realities of God's world are back down there on Everest . . . or, more likely yet, in the foothills and on the plains and in the teeming cities. Chimborazo is always "there," but we may have to live our whole lives "here."

Everest and Chimborazo: without too much straining, I think we may draw two truths for living from that comparison.

I

The first of them is: learn the satisfactions of where you are.

You can churn away an awful lot of energy always wishing you were somewhere else . . . remembering when you were younger or wishing you were older . . . angling for a more responsible job or pining for one with less pressure. But you can't *always* have Chimborazo. Everest, or even the foothills, may be all that's in the picture. So learn the satisfactions of where you are!

It's a good lesson for those of us who live in (or rather, endure through) Minnesota winters. Even when the calendar tries to convince us that spring can't be far behind, still it would be tempting to look for Chimborazo somewhere else. Down here on Everest they don't plow the streets in January or February because there might be a storm in December, and they don't plow in December because they say they spent the money in January or February. If we ever get a blizzard on the Fourth of July, I'm sure they'll really be ready with the plows, though! But, just when we Minnesotans began to despair, *National Geographic* came out with its beautiful picture of our place. *Fortune* magazine said,

"Once a monument to the nation's wealth and power, the big city in America has become a symbol of society's ailments—rampant crime in the streets, fiscal mismanagement, a deteriorating quality of life. But more and more often, any recitation of these urban failures ends up with mention of a shining exception: Minneapolis. In a magic sort of way, that city has taken on a cloak of glamour as the place where a lot of things are going right."[1]

Maybe Everest is all right after all . . . or even the foothills. Let others have their Chimborazo! We will learn the satisfactions of where we are! You can say that wherever you live.

We're dealing, of course, with implications far beyond the geographical ones. The Apostle Paul saw it long ago. He is in prison. Because of his Christian faith he has been jailed. He has been there for some time. He is anxiously awaiting the verdict which will mean life or death for him. The agony is enough to crush any one. But this man sends a letter to his Christian friends in the city of Phillipi. He says, ". . . stand firm . . . in the Lord, my beloved." And then, with an exercise in positive thinking that would make even Norman Vincent Peale blush:

". . . whatever is true, whatever is honorable, whatever is just, whatever is pure, whatever is lovely, whatever is gracious, if there is any excellence, if there is anything worthy of praise, think about these things."[2]

Now, from the comfort of your office or the luxury of your living room you might have written that. But *this* man has been languishing in prison! He lets us in on his secret. We learn the reason for his incredible serenity. He says, "I have learned, in whatever state I am, to be content."[3] He knows the difference between Everest and Chimborazo. He has learned the satisfactions of where he is. He goes on, ". . . in any and all circumstances I have learned the secret of facing plenty and hunger, abundance and want. I can do all things in him who strengthens me."[4] God is the source of his strength.

Paul believes you can have that strength, too. "My God," he says, "will supply every need of yours according to his riches in glory in Christ Jesus."[5] It is the strength to learn the satisfactions of where you are: the city where you are, the job where you are, the home where you are . . . the person you are. In America, we have always thought things were getting steadily and unceasingly better and better. We could have anything we set our minds to. With a little American spirit and the "man upstairs" on our side, we could have Chimborazo if we wanted it. We are learning that we may have to live with Everest, or even with the foothills. By God's grace we will learn that there are satisfactions there. One Church encouraged its people to learn a simpler lifestyle. It may not be either Everest or Chimborazo, but it would have its own intrinsic beauty:

Learn to like what does not cost much.

Learn to like reading, conversation, music.

Learn to like plain food, plain service, plain cooking.

Learn to like people, even though some of them may be very different from you.

Learn to keep your wants simple. Refuse to be owned and anchored by things and the opinions of others.

Learn to like the sunrise and the sunset, the beating of rain on the roof and windows and the gentle fall of snow in winter.

Learn to like life for its own sake.

What was Paul's word? "I have learned in whatever state I am, to be content." Learn the satisfactions of where you are!

II

A second truth for living comes to us as we stand in the shadow of Everest and Chimborazo: *be wherever God wants you to be.*

Sometimes it *is* Chimborazo . . . way up there on the peaks, where we give our best and live our noblest and strive for every possible quality of excellence. Apathy, after all, is not an especially Christian virtue. (Some people don't even care about finding out what that means!) There is a high road to be climbed and sometimes the word of God to an individual or to a Church or to a nation is like the word of a host to a guest who has taken the least honored seat: "Friend, come up higher."[6]

Where does God want you to be? What does He want you to do? Sometimes it is Chimborazo . . . and sometimes it's Everest or the foothills or way out on the prairies. In God's good world, one is not better than the other . . . just different. Or, we may put it this way: God does not call us always to be successful but to be faithful. We are not always to be perched up there on Chimborazo, but wherever God sets us down, we are to be faithful.

Not successful, but faithful. There was the Apostle Peter, the disciple who denied the Lord, but who came back in high devotion. Finally, according to tradition, he was crucified for his faith. But he asked to be crucified upside-down, for he felt himself unworthy even to die in the same manner as his Lord.

Not successful, but faithful. There was Martin Luther, a poor and humble monk, called before all the power and the pageantry of the Empire, pressured by all the compulsion of the Church. In spite of all, he stood firm in the conviction that Christ had called him to be faithful. He declared, "Here I stand! I cannot do otherwise. God help me. Amen!"

Not successful, but faithful. And that's the call for you and me. Not first of all to success but to faithfulness. Not always Chimborazo but always to faithfulness. When I was finishing my first pastorate, I thought that my achievements were obvious enough that I ought now to be appointed to one of the larger Churches in some clearly strategic situation. I went to a town you *literally can't drive through*. It's at the end of a road in a northern Minnesota forest. The only thing you can do is turn around and come back. By no means was it Chimborazo. It wasn't even Everest, but it *was* a place where I was called to be faithful. We learned to love the town and the people there. God, in His majesty and with the quiet brush of His Spirit, was there over and over again.

We're called to be faithful wherever we are . . . Chimborazo or Everest, Honolulu or Minneapolis. There's a scene in "The Wizard of Oz" in which the Tin Woodsman, and the Scarecrow are talking. "Have you any brains?" inquired the Scarecrow. "No, my head is quite empty," answered the Tin Woodsman, "but once I had brains, and a heart also; so, having tried them both, I should much rather have a heart." Well, I'm sure God wants us to use our brains but this also rings with clear, incessant truth: God needs the faithful, serving heart. Wherever you are, He needs it.

At the age of 47, the late Catholic monk, Thomas Merton said:

"I think sometimes that I may soon die, though I am not yet old. I don't know exactly what kind of conviction this thought carries with it or what I mean by it. Death is always a possibility for everyone. . . . So I have a habitual awareness that I may die, and that, if this is God's will, then I am glad. 'Go ye forth to meet Him.' And in the light of this I realize the futility of my cares and preoccupations . . . If I am not fully free, then the love of God, I hope, will free me. The important thing is simply turning to Him daily and often, preferring His will and His mystery to everything that is evidently and tangibly 'mine'."

49

Death—for any of us—may come while we still look at Chimborazo or Everest, or even the foothills, from afar. And that's all right. It may not be our desiring but it's all right, for God will still hold us in the hollow of his hand. The important thing—in all the moments of life or in the hour of death, on Chimborazo or Everest or in the block where you live: the important thing, as Merton says, ". . . is simply turning to God daily and often, preferring His will . . . to everything that is . . . mine."

References

1. Breckenfeld, Gurney; "Minneapolis: The Shining Exception"; in *Fortune*; January 1976; reprinted in *Mineapolis Star*; January 29, 1976; p. 8A.
2. Philippians 4:1,8.
3. Philippians 4:21.
4. Philippians 4:12-13.
5. Philippians 4:19.
6. Luke 14:10.

Established in the Faith
Can you give the
Christian family some guidelines?

Exodus: 3:1-6; II Timothy 1:3-7

Dick Van Dyke tells the story of a boy whose puppy had died. The lad was told it would be all right to say a brief prayer for it. That night he talked to God on the puppy's behalf:

"God, please take care of Sandy. He was a good dog. He never bit anyone. He never bothered the neighbors. He never wasted any food at mealtime. He never disobeyed. He always came when we called him. In fact, we all think he behaved better than anyone else in the family. Amen."[1]

I guess it's the question of how well the family is behaving that leads us to the next "hard question of faith." A whole batch of questions, really, but boiling down to this: *Can you give the Christian family some guidelines?*

That was an easier question for me twenty years ago. I was an expert then: I didn't have any children! As a matter of fact, then I had four perfect theories about raising children. Now I have four children—and no theories!

So I do not turn to the hard questions about children, youth, and the family as an "expert." There's a shattering sense in which we *all* "muddle through" when it comes to the various opportunities and crises of family living.

I can't rub my magic lantern and produce a genie who has "Seven Rules That Will Work For Every Family." Life is obviously more complex than that. I want, instead to do just two things which I trust will at least be thought-provoking. First: draw some lessons

51

from the Sacrament of Baptism. Second: suggest some themes for family living.

I

The Sacrament of Baptism is one of the Church's uniquely family-oriented celebrations. It has something to teach us.

A

It speaks to *parents*. It speaks rather insistently. It asks them to renew their own confession of Christian faith. It calls on them to acknowledge the power of their own example: to lead "a life that becomes the gospel." It demands their promise that they will exert specifically Christian guidance, *all godly care* that this child be brought up in the Christian faith . . . be taught the holy Scriptures . . . learn to give reverent attendance upon both public and private worship . . . be kept under the ministry and guidance of the Church. *Man alive*! If all that were illegal and we who have ever brought a child for holy baptism were arrested for making good on our promises, do you think there would be enough evidence to convict us?

The Sacrament of Baptism zeroes in on parents. It talks with a voice that has sounded for thousands of years. Most of us know the familiar story of the burning bush and the call to Moses to lead his people. The God who speaks in the decisive moment recalls the rich heritage which has been handed to Moses: "*I am the God of your father*, the God of Abraham, the God of Isaac, and the God of Jacob."[2] We may give our children fine insurance policies and top-flight educations, and trips to far-away places and remember them well in our wills—but we will have denied them the one heritage that finally matters most if the good Lord cannot say convincingly to them, "I am the God of your father . . . and of your mother." The Apostle Paul's young friend Timothy could claim such an endowment. Paul said to him, "I am reminded of your sincere faith, a faith that dwelt first in your grandmother Lois and your mother Eunice and now, I am sure, dwells in you."[3]

Baptism speaks to parents and asks them to hand on that kind of heritage.

But the baptismal vows do not stop with the parents. They move on to include the entire Church as a partner in the whole exciting venture. Every last one of us who is a part of the company of faith runs the risk of indictment after every baptism.

"With God's help we will so order our lives after the example of Christ, that this child, surrounded by steadfast love, may be established in the faith, and confirmed and strengthened in the way that leads to life eternal."[4]

"Surrounded by steadfast love"—not only of the parents, you see . . . but of a whole caring congregation. In other days, there were always sponsors or godparents at a baptism. Sometimes there still are. But not always . . . and the reason is that the whole Church takes the responsibility. Each child who is baptized has a whole sanctuary full of godparents. They *all* promise to surround the baptized person with steadfast love—to create and develop . . . and be . . . the kind of Church where little children and young people can in fact grow up and be "established in the faith."

A guideline for the Christian family: take seriously all that baptism means.

II

Well, that all sounds like beautiful music! Ask your tough questions about children and youth and the intricacies of family living and get a couple of tunes about the implications of baptism and Zap! You've got it! But it's not that easy. Everyone knows that the music of family life is sometimes beautiful, but other times ugly; sometimes quiet and soothing, but other times loud and painful to our ears; sometimes a grand and thrilling symphony, but other times a dischordant mess. When it is ugly or loud or dischordant, our natural question is "What did we do wrong?" But that's not always a very productive question. "What do we do now?" is the essential one. Past mistakes and previous accomplishments may, of course, teach us something but they cannot be re-lived. What happened last week or last month or last year or fifteen years ago cannot be done over. So let us learn—but let us not languish there. "What do we do now?" is the essential question.

What themes can we write into the score of family living?

A

There is the theme of *individuality*. A poet said it this way:

> He's not group conscious? So . . . he's not.
> He wasn't even as a tot.
> And now that he is ten years old,
> I can't see why he must be told
> Repeatedly and yet again
> He *must* play like all boys of ten.
>
> Why should he think their thoughts, I beg,
> Perhaps he's Einstein in the egg.
> Why *must* a child be in the coup
> If he's not wedded to the group?
> There should be room, it seems to me,
> For individuality.[5]

That says something, I think, about the way we love our children
. . . . as individuals: not only accepting but nurturing and developing their own strong points and keen interests until they have become the fully unique persons that God Himself intended. Out of another culture and faith, Kahlil Gibran instructs us in *The Prophet*: "Your children are not your children. They are the sons and daughters of Life's longing for itself. They come through you but not from you, and though they are with you yet they belong not to you . . . You may house their bodies but not their souls, for their souls dwell in the house of tomorrow, which you cannot visit, not even in your dreams. You may strive to be like them, but seek not to make them like you."[6]

B

Individuality is one theme. *Guidance* is another. The development of individuality does not mean that we abdicate our responsibility for guiding. Remember those baptismal vows? To exercise "all godly care . . . ." That's guidance!

Two boys were standing on a street corner one night. The first one said, "I have to go home" "How come?" asked the second. "Because my parents said I had to be home by midnight." And the second replied, "I wish my parents would tell me I have to come home." The lack of a guiding hand was interpreted to mean there was no hand that cared, either. Obviously there is no way to guarantee that our children will always follow the standards we choose, but at the very least they have the right to know what our standards are . . . and why we have chosen them.

A seed planted in the ground has to do its own growing—to be responsible, as it were, for itself. It needs to become an individual plant. But it needs help. Someone else has to be there with light and warmth and enrichment and the removal of the weeds. Individuality, yes . . . but with loving and responsible guidance.

Can the development of a person be any different?

C

I don't know any one word for the next theme but its idea is, "*Parents are people too!*" The nurturing of the individuality of our children in no way calls for us to give up our own individuality. As early in life as possible, and repeatedly throughout the years, children need to learn that their parents, too, have hopes and dreams, needs and emotions. In short: parents are people. Kids are sometimes crabby and need to be left alone—but parents get crabby, too—and tired and emotional. They have responsibilities and plans and it is no sign of responsible parenthood to let anyone else, even their own children, tromp all over them.

In the same passage from *The Prophet* to which I have already referred, Gibran compares parents and children to bows and arrows. Parents are the bows from which children as living arrows are sent swift and far. There is a Master Archer, so Gibran says,

> "Let your bending in the Archer's hand be for gladness;
> For even as he loves the arrow that flies, so He loves also
> the bow that is stable."[7]

Parents are people, too.

D

One final theme: the theme of love. There's a lot of "muddling" in this business of family living, but I still believe that what will see us through, somehow, is the old quality called "love." Certain surveys have asked parents if they would have children if they had it to do over again. I wish the polltakers would find something constructive to do with their time, but I guess the surveys have at least this positive aspect: it reminds parents who are having problems that they are far from alone.

In the midst of those problems, in the midst of all the grittiness as well as the glory of family living, I point you to the supreme theme of love. It is a love, through Jesus, which can patch up and heal and renew what we, in our clumsiness, goof up. Betty Ford has been widely quoted and frequently misquoted. We may have missed her statement about what our reactions should be when our children's behavior violates our own standards. She said,

". . . this must never cause us to withdraw the love, the counseling, and the understanding that they need now, more than ever before. This is the essence of responsible parenthood."[8]

Call it sentimental if you wish, but I believe in the love which the New Testament[9] describes as patient and kind, not jealous or boastful, not arrogant or rude, not irritable or resentful . . . love which rejoices in the right and bears, believes, hopes, and endures all things . . . love which, along with faith and hope, abides forever: I believe in such love as the ultimate guideline for the family. Held ever before us as a goal and beneath us as a sustaining power, made visible in all our day-by-day decisions, it will be what finally holds not only the family but the Church and society itself together. *Sound that theme always!*

References

1. Van Dyke, Dick; *Faith, Hope, and Hilarity*; (quoted in Kennedy, Gerald; *My Third Reader's Notebook*; p. 137).

2. Exodus 3:6.

3. II Timothy 1:5.

4. Baptism ritual, United Methodist Church.

5. Antolini, Margaret Fishback; (quoted in Kennedy, Gerald; *A Second Reader's Notebook*; p. 188).

6. Gibran, Kahlil; *The Prophet*; p. 21.

7. *Ibid.*, p. 22.

8. *Edina Sun*; October 1, 1975; p. 6 (in letter to Mrs. John F. Jundin).

9. I Corinthians 13.

Forgiveness as a Style of Life
How far does forgiveness go?
If I am forgiven, am I also held responsible?

Ephesians 4:25-32

A faithful friend of my congregation had some rather important things to do one Sunday morning. He asked me what the penance would be if he missed Church. He had me on the spot—since the sermon was going to deal with forgiveness!

It is alleged that a certain minister recently reported to his congregation that there is a total of 726 sins. His telephone rang all week with people asking for copies of the list!

One night in early spring we had a beautiful rain and when we woke up the next morning, the sun was shining. The world had been cleansed—as if all the sins of winter had been washed away.

Sin and forgiveness: our next "hard question of faith" asks, "How far does forgiveness go?" There are, as usual, a whole batch of tough questions:

How can we be held responsible for the consequences of our actions and yet be forgiven for our actions?

How can the sins of the fathers be felt by many yet unborn children if God forgives sin and removes them from us as far as the east is from the west?

How can a person hold to his concepts and beliefs and still be forgiving of others and their actions and beliefs?

How does a Christian respond to the negative behavior of others? "Turn the other cheek" does not seem effective. "Seventy times seven" is beyond most humans' capacity.

How does a Christian deal with guilt?

How far does forgiveness go?

57

Let's respond to all that by taking a probing look at *forgiveness as a style of life*.

I

I have to ask you, first of all, to take a Biblical look at forgiveness in the context of life. Use the New Testament Letter to the Ephesians as an illustration. The text for our thinking is Paul's word there: ". . . be kind to one another, tenderhearted, forgiving one another, as God in Christ forgave you."[1]

That comes at the end of the fourth chapter. Paul has been leading up to it. The chapter begins with his saying, "*I therefore* . . . ." Whenever, in the Bible you read the word "therefore" always ask what it's there for! Quite clearly, in this case, Paul's "therefore" points us back to an earlier idea. We think immediately of his famous statement in the second chapter, his summary of God's love acting in our lives: ". . . by grace you have been saved through faith . . . ."[2]

"*I therefore* . . . beg you to lead a life worthy of the calling to which you have been called, with all lowliness and meekness, with patience, forbearing one another in love . . . ."[3] The rest of the Letter spells out what that kind of life—a life motivated by God's loving grace—looks like. Later he is to say, ". . . be imitators of God, as beloved children. And walk in love, as Christ loved us . . . ."[4]

Plunked down in the center of all that is a sweeping series of ethical admonitions:

> ". . . putting away falsehood . . . speak the truth . . . for we are members one of another . . . Be angry but do not sin; do not let the sun go down on your anger . . . Let all bitterness and wrath and anger and clamor and slander be put away from you . . ."[5]

And then: ". . . be kind to one another, tenderhearted, forgiving one another, as God in Christ forgave you."

Forgiveness, then, is no isolated rule. It makes its best sense as one golden thread woven into a whole fabric of living. It is part of a style of life. Most so-called "alternative lifestyles" come off as not much more than rationalizations for "I'm going to do what I feel like doing." Paul, as a follower of Jesus, is offering a style of

58

life which is an alternative to bitterness and anger, grudge-bearing and resentment. Its keystone is: ". . . be kind to one another, tenderhearted, forgiving one another, as God in Christ forgave you."

II

Forgiveness is a style of life. But there are some hard questions about that. We turn to them now. They are questions like: Is forgiveness beyond human ability? What about the consequences of my actions? Why should I keep trying?

A

Is forgiveness beyond human ability? It sounds nice, sure, but isn't it really an impractical ideal? Well, of course, we don't always reach it. We are human and we always fall short. When, as Luke's Gospel records it, Jesus was talking with his friends about forgiveness, their overwhelmed response was, "Increase our faith!"[6] They knew their weakness. And we know ours. But two things need to be said.

One of them is that it's important to remember that we have been forgiven first. "Be kind . . . tenderhearted . . . forgiving . . . *as God in Christ forgave you* . . ." The Biblical evidence surely is that only the forgiving spirit can receive God's forgiveness. He will not jam His love down our unwilling throats: "Forgive us our trespasses, *as we forgive* . . . ." But the point remains: God is not asking us to do something He has not already done. Our forgiveness is a mirror of His forgiveness. We rely on God's mercy, even before we are asked to be merciful. An epitaph in a novel by George MacDonald catches the spirit:

> "Here lie I, Martin Elginbrodde;
> Hae mercy o' my soul, Lord God;
> As I wad do, were I Lord God,
> An' ye were Martin Elginbrodde."[7]

Confronted with the difficult if not impossible task of forgiveness, we recall that we have been forgiven first. We are to be merciful because we have received mercy.

Then this also needs to be said: the immensely difficult is held up as an ideal for us even when we do not reach it. Peter came to

Jesus one day and asked, "Lord, how often shall my brother sin against me, and I forgive him? As many as seven times?" We can imagine Jesus shaking His head at this poor disciple, so much like ourselves, who always kept trying but somehow never quite seemed to understand. Jesus said, "No, Peter, not seven times. Seventy times seven!"[8] *Peter understood* the human limitations, the daily realities you and I struggle with, the question, "Isn't forgiveness beyond human ability?" "How many times do I have to forgive this crumb-bum? Seven times? That's a lot, but I might be able to struggle through and make it." *But Jesus knew* the attraction of Divine appeal, the magnetic drawing power of an ideal that makes us stretch. He wanted to liberate Peter from the kind of skimpy love that gets measured out with an eyedropper: "One—two—three—four—five—six—seven! There!" Not that! Love freely poured until you cannot count the drops . . . or even want to! Seventy times seven! Four-hundred-ninety: we can figure that out "in our heads." But Jesus is talking about a celestial arithmetic that you cannot do in your head. You lose track. You can only do it in your heart.

It may still be beyond our frail abilities. But it's an ideal that's a whole lot better than nursing the rancor and the bitterness that can eat away at our souls like a cancer. And when we fall, there is a forgiving God who understands and picks us up and sets us on our way again.

Is forgiveness beyond human ability? Maybe. But Jesus calls for us to reach for it anyhow.

B

We turn to another question: *If I am forgiven, am I also held responsible for the consequences of my actions?*

Maybe we can get at that if we recall briefly another of Paul's affirmations: "God was in Christ reconciling the world to himself, not counting their trespasses against them . . . ."[9] Paul is saying that God does not keep the record of our misdeeds on the awesome pages of some everlasting ledger book. From God's point of view, the things we have done—however evil—are blotted out as if they had never been. But that cannot annul all the consequences of what we have done. Health ruined by indulgence may be forever lost. Relationships that should never have started may be terminated but some of the effects will linger for a very long time. Our congregation "sponsored" a Cambodian refugee family. More accurately, we were given the opportunity of loving three beautiful people. We tried to help them rebuild their lives but, partly as a consequence of the actions of the United States in Cambodia and partly as a consequence of the actions of those who came to control the government there, it will be forever true that the lives of our new friends can never be the same again. We can repent, and I pray to God we will. We can be forgiven, and I have faith in God we will be, but there is simply no way to erase completely the disruption that has come to their lives.

What is different because we have been forgiven, then? If the consequences linger, isn't it pretty hollow to say that I have been forgiven? What is different is that we are no longer paralyzed by what we have done. Forgiveness may not always be able to undo what we have done. It *can* set us free to move on toward a new day. The consequences and the guilt, to put it another way, do not forever lock us out of the throne room of God's Love. He sends His son with the keys to the door. And when the penitent sinner knocks, the door swings open. We are not turned away. We stand here, blemished and imperfect. With the hymn writer, all we can really say is, "Just as I am . . . I come!"[10] To our astonishment, the word of welcome is for us! There is great joy in all the far corners of heaven over one sinner who repents![11]

C

One final question remains: *Why keep trying*? If I am going to be forgiven anyhow, what difference does it make what I do?

Well, of course, we may treat love flippantly like that if we wish. We may greet the "amazing grace" with which God meets us and spit in its face. We may, if we wish, live with a motto that says, "God loves me . . . and I don't care."

Or: we may take to heart the understanding that forgiveness is a style of life. After the Second World War, many people sent gifts to Displaced Persons in Europe. One woman sent a note with her gift, "Ten dollars I give in forgiveness of the German lad who by no fault of his own killed my son." We could live like that.

We could take to heart the rich and deep implications of John Greenleaf Whitter's lines:

61

"Dear Lord and Father of mankind,
Forgive our foolish ways;
Reclothe us in our rightful mind,
In purer lives thy service find,
In deeper reverence, praise."[12]

We could take to heart the incisive understanding that the Cross which stands at the center of life sounds ever and again the message that God in Christ forgave us. It is in the shadow of that Cross that we, in return, are asked to forgive.

A little boy got lost in London one day. A policeman—a "bobby"—found him and asked where he lived. "I don't know," he cried, "but if you'll take me to the top of the hill where the white Cross stands, I can find my way from there!" Forgiveness as a style of life: it's a challenging goal. By ourselves it is impossible. But from the top of the hill where the Cross stands, we may at last find our way. The road sign on that hill reads: ". . . be kind . . . be tenderhearted . . . forgiving . . . as God in Christ forgave you."

References

1. Ephesians 4:32.
2. Ephesians 2:8.
3. Ephesians 4:1-2.
4. Ephesians 5:1-2.
5. Ephesians 4:25-31.
6. Luke 17:5.
7. MacDonald, George; in *David Elginbrod*; (quoted in *Interpreter's Bible*; volume 7; p. 328).
8. Matthew 18:21-22.
9. II Corinthians 5:19.
10. *The Methodist Hymnal*; No. 119.
11. Luke 15:7.
12. *The Methodist Hymnal*; No. 235.

You Pack Your Own Chute
Can faith help rearrange my life?
When I try to improve,
why do the negative aspects intensify?

Romans 7:15-25

Peter Marshall once said, "We need a faith that is as real as fire . . . and prayer as real as potatoes."[1] The heat of a fire and the reality of potatoes we can understand. *Faith* is something else again. Sometimes it's as airy as the winds of March, or as fluffy as cotton candy at the State Fair. But when we ask the next "hard question of faith" we want something *as real as potatoes*: Can faith help me rearrange my life? And when I try the rearranging, why do things seem to get worse?

The Apostle Paul would have understood the question. He knew the dilemma behind it. "I do not understand my own actions," he said. "For I do not do what I want, but I do the very thing I hate."[2] His life needed rearranging. Some scholars have contended that such a confession had to be Paul's reflections on his life before he was a Christian. But every morally sensitive person, Christian or not, knows what he's talking about. "I do not understand my own actions." The struggle is human! The Christian is not exempt from it. Like everyone else, we sometimes feel as uncomfortable with our lives as a porcupine rolled up the wrong way.

What, then, of faith? How can we experience it in a more concrete way? Can it help us improve ourselves? Make us more successful? Can it enable us to control the circumstances instead of being controlled by them? Can we really apply it? In ways as real as potatoes? Can faith rearrange our lives?

63

We may respond in at least three ways and the first of them is this: *When you want to rearrange your life, faith says, "You pack your own chute."*

That way of putting it comes from a provocative little movie. A certain woman is afraid of heights and particularly afraid of parachuting. She determines that she must overcome these irrational fears. (Personally, when it comes to the fear of parachuting, I'll be content to go my whole life without conquering that irrationality!) At any rate, she struggles with her fear. She is told that the parachute will protect her. "But how," she wants to know, "can I be sure the chute will open?" And she is told, "You know—because you pack your own chute. You don't depend on someone else. You take responsibility for your own chute."

The implications of that are obvious. They go far beyond parachuting. You pack your own life: you don't blame someone else for the way it's put together. The attempt to squirm out of that responsibility is not something you and I invented this morning. Adam and Eve were the first squirmers. They were still licking their chops from that delicious fruit when the Lord God confronted them. Adam was right in there with his answer: "The woman you gave me, she gave me the fruit . . . ." He put two giant steps between himself and any sense of responsibility. One step: the woman! Two steps: the woman *You* gave me! Eve was pretty good at squirming, too: the serpent You put here . . . he talked me into it! Someone else packed the chute!

No, says the word of faith: if you're serious about rearranging your life, you pack your own chute! You take responsibility for your own life. Some friends brought a paralytic man to Jesus. Seeing their faith, He said to the man, "Your sins are forgiven . . . Take up your bed and walk."[3]

Now I don't know *how* Jesus accomplished that or, with absolutely unshakeable certainty, *if* He did. But this I do believe: the essential point is that Jesus can release us from the things that paralyze our spirits. Then, no matter how our bodies creak along, we can—in the sense that finally matters—"take up our *lives* and run!" The paralytic man had to take some responsibility for himself, though. Jesus could speak the liberating words, "Your sins are forgiven!", but only the man himself could put the liberation into action: "Take up your bed and walk!"

So with us. The paralysis of having had inadequate parents or a poor childhood or bad schools, the paralysis of living in a shattering kind of Watergate world threatened by a nuclear clock not far from midnight: it's all there, and we can let it make spiritual and moral cripples of us forever. Or, as of this particular date in this particular year, we can decide to listen—way down deep inside ourselves—to what Jesus was really talking about. We can hear Him for ourselves: "Take up your life and walk!" Jess Lair, in his little volume, *I Ain't Much Baby, But I'm All I've Got*, quotes one of his students: "For what I am today, shame on my parents. But if I stay that way, shame on me."[4]

You pack your own chute. If you want to rearrange your life, that's one of the first words of faith.

II

A second word that faith speaks is, "You don't do your own thing."

You pack your own chute but the paradox is that you can't do it alone. Someone else made the parachute and you go up in a plane someone else built and you take off from a runway someone else laid down and the breakfast you ate before you got to the airport was from food someone else grew and harvested. We're interrelated and dependent on other people. And they depend on us. We're all "people who need people." A small child in his upstairs bedroom was frightened by a thunderstorm late one night. His mother came up and, trying to reassure him, said "Don't be afraid. God is up here with you and will take care of you." "Well," said the little fellow, "you can stay up here with God. I'm going downstairs and sleep with Daddy!"

Our lives are interwoven with other people. The world isn't put together in such a way that we can go our merry individual ways. Some people have never gotten over Galileo's discovery that the earth is not the stationary center around which the whole rest of the universe revolves. They still think the earth stands in its fixed place while the sun makes its daily journey from East to West.

Worse yet, they think that they personally are the center around which the rest of the world is to revolve.

Oh, they don't put it quite that baldly. They find a nice toupeé to cover it up with. They drag out some cute little mottoes like, "Get it all together. If it feels good, do it. Do your own thing."

By contrast, in a significant little book called, *The Pain of Being Human*, Eugene Kennedy calls us to acceptance of responsibility, saying:

> ". . . self-examination is a difficult task, one that requires searching honesty and self-discipline as well as the ability to balance one's own inclinations against the rights and needs of other persons . . . The mature person . . . perhaps a dozen or more times a day, does things that in some way or other he does not feel like doing. That is to say, he is grown up rather than hung-up on making the universe spin around his own personality."[5]

When you would rearrange your life, faith points you to the hard realities of responsibility. It says, "You don't do your own thing."

III

Then a third word. The first was, "You pack your own chute." The second was, "You don't do your own thing." *And the third: "God will work with you."*

"When I try to improve," we ask, "why do the negative things in my life get worse?" The agony is real. Paul's cry was, "I do not do what I want, but I do the very thing I hate." A wrenching outburst came next: "Wretched man that I am! Who will deliver me from this body of death?" But from there he moved to an exclamation of faith: "Thanks be to God through Jesus Christ our Lord!"[6]

Was he just being pious?

There's far more than piety here. Paul has glimpsed the truth that in the rearranging of our lives God will work with us. A line in his letter to the Philippians helps clarify his thinking. There he says, ". . . work out your own salvation with fear and trembling; for God is at work in you . . ."[7] That's the perplexing language of paradox, but it's also the stuff of reality. "Work out your own salvation: God is at work with you."

God makes moral demands . . . and then gives us what is demanded. It is a two-fold working of our will and of His will.

We are not left to rearrange our lives by ourselves. We work . . . but God works with us. One writer put it this way:

"I sail my boat, yet not I but the winds of God that are with me; I grow my vegetables, yet not I but the growing power which nature supplies; I start my car, yet not I but the electrical power that was here before cars were invented. In all these ways we work, and yet the working is not all ours—but we must work. . . ."[8]

The rearranging of our lives? We pack our own chute. But with a strength not our own.

Faith as real as potatoes? Only God makes potatoes grow. But we do the planting and the cultivating.

References

1. Marshall, Peter; *Mr. Jones, Meet the Master*; p. 176.
2. Romans 7:15.
3. Matthew 9:1-8.
4. Lair, Jess; *I Ain't Much, Baby—But I'm All I've Got*; p. 39.
5. Kennedy, Eugene; *The Pain of Being Human*; p. 68.
6. Romans 7:15, 24-25.
7. Philippians 2:12-13.
8. *Interpreter's Bible*; volume 11; pp. 55-56.

In Defense of Some Old-Fashioned Ideas
Does the Christian have something
to say about sex, love, and marriage?

I Corinthians 13:1-7

Church people need to be current, up-to-date, relevant, aware that the only world we've been given to live in is a contemporary world. We need to know what the day's headlines are.

The other side of the need for freshness, however, is the need for stability. Contemporaneity (if you'll forgive such a big word) needs always to be balanced with some sense of the eternal. The slow march of the centuries has something to say to the quick passing of the hours. Back in 1952 when Lillian Hellman was called before the House Un-American Activities Committee, she decided she would tell them whatever they asked about her own activities. She would refuse, however, to testify against other people. She gave her reason in this telling sentence: "I cannot and will not cut my conscience to fit this year's fashions . . ."[1]

In all of life, "this year's fashions" are something, but they are decidely not everything. Thus, I invite you to look with me beyond the flabby flexibility of this week's trends. Sex and love and marriage may, rather obviously, be lived at the level of the latest idea, but I believe with passionate conviction that some of the old-fashioned ideas point us to what the Apostle Paul had in mind when he introduced his immortal poem on love by saying he would show us "a more excellent way."[2]

I

Consider this old-fashioned idea first: *sex is a sacred symbol.* The idea is around, and I suppose it always has been, that sex is primarily a physical thing. "It's pleasurable and there's nothing wrong with pleasure and if I can enjoy myself, why not? And if there's a little love involved, that makes it right, so long as nobody gets hurt."

So goes the argument, and it sounds rather nice . . . until we take it apart. Sex is, of course, physical, and the Christian ideal joins most of the rest of the world in affirming that it is meant to be pleasurable. But any clear-headed understanding person also knows that it is far more than physical: our whole personalities get involved, and are not very easily extricated. Further, when we start with "love makes it right," the problem is figuring out what we mean by the word, "love." It has so many associations with romance and with emotion. I'm in favor of romance and emotion but they are experts at fogging up our brains. And justification of our actions on the *negative* basis of "so long as nobody gets hurt" has to strain pretty hard to be a Christian justification. We are committed, as those who take the name of Christ, to *positive* principles, to the enhancement of persons. Jesus would have a hard time agreeing, I think, that love means "so long as nobody gets hurt." Richard Hettlinger, a college teacher and counselor, has written a book whose very title is a provocative reminder. He calls it, *Sex Isn't That Simple*. In it, he says,

"Whenever a decision or choice is to be made concerning behavior, the moral decision will be the one which works toward the creation of trust, confidence, and integrity in relationships."[3]

So what are we saying? That sex is physical, of course, and we thank God for that. But we are also saying that there is "a more excellent way." We begin to walk that way if we understand that *sex is symbolic*. Think of sex as any physical expression of affection. A boy and girl hold hands and it means, "I like you." The hand-holding is a symbol of that liking. A boy and girl kiss and it means, "I like you very much." The kiss is a symbol of that liking-very-much. So it is with all the physical expressions of affection until we come to the most intimate one of all, sexual intercourse, which at its highest means, "I love you with all that I am. I commit myself to you without reservation." The ultimate sex act is a symbol of that love and that commitment.

There are appropriate symbols and inappropriate ones. If I meet you for the first time, a handshake is an appropriate symbol;

throwing my arms around you is inappropriate: it would be trying to symbolize too much. We may, of course, let our sexual symbols mean very little if we choose. Or, stirred on by the call to a "more excellent way," we may choose to symbolize all our affections joyfully but appropriately. Then, love's fullest physical symbol will be reserved for that situation in which we have fully and without reserve committed ourselves to another, for better or for worse.

Sex is a marvelous gift. I call you to the old-fashioned idea that it is, at its best, a sacred symbol to be treated with care and tenderness and clear-headed thoughtfulness.

II

See also a second old-fashioned idea: *love takes hard work*. Nowhere in all literature is there a more eloquent description of love than in Paul's poem beginning, "If I speak in the tongues of men and of angels, but have not love . . ." It is, however, not a description of an emotion. It's not ethereal and airy. It does not tell about that feeling you feel like you're going to feel when you feel like you're going to feel a feeling you've never felt like feeling before. That's puppy love: the problem is it can lead to a dog's life!

The Christian Gospel, and Paul in his immortal description, understands that love is not primarily a matter of how you feel: love is first of all a matter of what you do. When love is a feeling it does a lot of gonging and clanging but when the drummer gets tired the sound fades away. Love in a deeper sense, the love which abides and does not evaporate with the morning mist,

> ". . . is patient and kind . . . not jealous or boastful; it is not arrogant or rude. Love does not insist on its own way; it is not irritable or resentful; it does not rejoice at wrong, but rejoices in the right. Love bears all things, believes all things, hopes all things, endures all things."[4]

J. B. Phillipps translates like this: "Love is not touchy. It does not compile statistics of evil or gloat over the wickedness of other people . . . Love knows no limit to its endurance, no end to its trust, no fading of its hope. . . ."

Obviously, we have here the description of an ideal. In our humanness, we do not attain it. We reach with arms of loving under-

70

standing to those for example, for whom there was no way but the road of divorce. But that does not obliterate the goal of working at love. No one in his right mind ever told us that loving was going to be easy. Love takes work. Every human relationship, including every marriage, would be strengthened and beautified by that understanding.

Father Eugene Kennedy in his helpful little volume, *The Pain of Being Human*, says it this way:

> "Love's labor is involved in perserving at the effort to understand another even after you think you have heard everything he has to say. The work of love is hard indeed when it demands that we overcome our tendency to turn inside ourselves when we are hurt. It is hard work to try to be vital and responsive to another when we are tired and would just as soon be left alone. Love is very demanding of the best of our energies in moments of tension and misunderstanding with those we love. We are tempted to let all that is hostile bubble up at those moments, and it is hard work to face our anger and to keep it from destroying our love."[5]

Love takes work, but work, as Kahlil Gibran put it, is "love made visible."[6]

III

We've looked at two old-fashioned ideas: "Sex is a sacred symbol" and "Love takes hard work." Then this third: *marriage is still beautiful.*

It is not the only beautiful thing. The fulfillment of life may surely be found by persons who, by circumstances or by choice, never marry or who are not now married. Women's Liberation is teaching us what the Christian faith at its best has always known, but has sometimes forgotten: that you don't have to be married to be a full person. And, as I have said, we may understand with deep compassion those who have gone through the pain and the agony of a marriage that didn't work.

Nevertheless we may affirm that marriage is beautiful. The divorce statistics might tell us otherwise, but they tend to hide as much as they reveal. They do not tell us that 66% of married couples stay together for life. They do not tell us that because of earlier marriages and longer life spans those who stay together do so for longer years than ever before. They do not tell us that 80% of those divorced think highly enough of marriage to remarry within five years.[7]

There is still something beautiful about marriage. Marriages are not made in heaven: they come in kits and we have to put them together, but they are beautiful. With all the ups and downs of the years, a couple may grow in grace and in understanding. One grandmother on her Golden Wedding told the secret of her happy marriage. "On my wedding day," she said, "I decided to make a list of ten of my husband's faults which, for the sake of our marriage, I would overlook." Someone asked her what the faults were. "To tell you the truth," she said, "I never did get around to listing them. But whenever he did something that made me mad, I would just say to myself, 'Lucky for him that's one of the ten!'"

In her own way, she understood, I think, what the marriage ritual means when it calls marriage a *covenant*. It is not a contract. In a contract, the minute one party does not live up to every letter of the agreement, it may be torn up. A contract is a 50/50 proposition. A covenant is a 100/100 matter. It knows that there will be strains and stresses in the relationship, but it holds on. Paul says it "endures all things." It does not crawl its way to the half-way mark and wait for the other person to get there. In free abandon and with joyful disregard of all the tiny little measurements, it meets the other person wherever he or she happens to be.

In the Old Testament story, when the people of Israel had been in the wilderness a long time and they were very hungry, suddenly one morning there was a flaky substance on the ground. It was a sort of bread. They called it manna from heaven. There was plenty for everyone, but they were not allowed to store it up and hoard it for another day. Some of them disregarded the rules and tried to keep some for themselves. By the next day it was wormy and had turned sour.[8]

The manna was evidence of the love of God. It was not to be stored up, lest it turn sour. So it is with marriage, stored love turns stale. To see marriage as a covenant is to see a love which does not hold back, waiting for the inchy little measurements of the other's worthiness. Stored love turns stale. A couple, in sacred covenant, makes a pledge of faith to love, honor, and keep each other. In. sickness and in health, for better or for worse, for richer or for poorer, they love and cherish each other until in the depths of their beings they know for themselves that marriage is beautiful.

Then, finally, just this overarching word. We are those who take the name of Christ as our own. Whether we are young and mostly looking forward, or immersed somewhere in the middle of life's years, or older and mostly looking at gloried memories: to take the name of Christ is to seek to live the life of love in all its deepest and highest dimensions. "By this will all men know that you are my disciples," He said, "that you love one another." And His great apostle reminds that enduring forever are faith, hope, and love. But the greatest of all is love.

References

1. Quoted, *Time*; May 10, 1976; p. 83 (in a review of Lillian Hellman's book, *Scoundrel Time*).

2. I Corinthians 12:31.

3. Hettlinger, Richard; *Sex Isn't That Simple: The New Sexuality on Campus*; p. 115.

4. I Corinthians 13:4-7.

5. Kennedy, Eugene; *The Pain of Being Human*; p. 171.

6. Gibran, Kahlil; *The Prophet*; p. 33.

7. See articles by Michael Novak in *Minneapolis Tribune*, May 2, 1976, pp. 1E to 8E, and by Sam Keen in *Family Circle*, May 1976; pp. 25-32.

8. Exodus 16:13-21.

He Who Comes in the Name of the Lord
A Sermon for Palm Sunday
Is Jesus essential?
What about other religions?

Matthew 21:1-11; John 13:34-35; 14:6, 9

"Who is this?"[1] The New Testament never takes an answer to that Palm Sunday question, puts it in a box, wraps it in pretty paper, and ties a red ribbon around it for us. "Who is this?" Oh, there are lots of titles: prophet, Savior, Lord, Son of God, Son of Man . . . about forty-two of them if you really want to make a whole list. "Who is this?" The Palm Sunday crowd cried, "Blessed is he who comes in the name of the Lord!"[2]

What does that mean? We look at Him and continue to ask our "hard question of faith." "How can we be sure that Christ is God and not just 'very godly'? What about those who worhip a God through other religions? If Jesus lived today, would He teach the same things?" And the central question: *"Is Jesus essential?"*

The New Testament writers threw away all the pretty paper and the red ribbons—and all the nifty little answers. When they went to tell us who Jesus *is* they just had to point to what He *did*. They didn't write a systematic theology; they just tried to describe their experience. Out of that experience, they saw, for one thing, Jesus as Lord; for another, Jesus as one who revealed the Father; and for a third, Jesus as one who inspired love. We may, I think, push toward some answer to the "hard questions" about Him if we look at each of those experiences in turn.

I

First: the New Testament experience is that Jesus is Lord.

74

Few people in the twentieth century have explained the Scriptures with greater clarity than the Scottish writer, William Barclay. He outlines ten shadings of meaning in the one New Testament word, "Lord." There is a sweep from a title of respect similar to our "Sir," to the owner of a piece of property; from a master as opposed to slave, to the head of a household; from the guardian of one who has no legal rights, to the emperor and finally, to God Himself. Then Barclay draws it all together and brings it home this way:

> "If I call Jesus Lord I ought to mean that he is the undisputed owner of my life, that he is the master whose slave I am, that he is the head of the great family in heaven and earth of which God is the Father, that he is the helper of the helpless and the protector of those who have no rights, that he has absolute direct authority over my actions, that I regard him as the king of my life, that I look upon him as divine, that he is intimately connected with the God whom I worship and adore."[3]

That's an overwhelming description, but that was the experience of the disciples: they were overwhelmed!

To take Him seriously is still overwhelming. To say Jesus is Lord is to say that no one else, no other thing, has equal status in our lives. To say Jesus is Lord is to limit all our other options. Compare it this way. A man taking a bride does not thereby say there is nothing good about any other woman. The woman getting married does not thereby put down all other men as worthless. But, from this day forward, no one else has equal status. There is a voluntary limiting of one's options. The wedding ritual says it when it asks, ". . . *forsaking* all others, (wilt thou) keep thee only unto her (or him) . . . ?"

In some similar way, to say "Jesus is Lord" is to limit our options. It is not to say there is no value in other religions. It is not, I think, to prohibit God from loving those who choose another way or who know nothing but some other way. That, surely, is His own decision. But it is to say, "*I* cannot forever go in all directions at once. *For me, Jesus is Lord.* Here is where I limit my options. For me, Jesus—not one of the yogis nor Buddha nor Uncle Sam nor money nor sex nor 'being my own person'—but *Jesus* is Lord. I may learn from other religions, I may study other philosophies, I may be inspired by the lives of other saints, but always there at the center is the Man from Nazareth." Once I have said, "Jesus is Lord," no one is His equal.

II

The New Testament experience led to a second truth: it is that Jesus reveals the Father.

As the Fourth Gospel tells His life story, Jesus makes some statements that have troubled a lot of people. They sound so audacious and exclusive: "No one comes to the Father except by me . . . He who has seen me has seen the Father."[4] The *Interpreter's Bible* says that this is ". . . without exception, surely the most staggering saying to be found in human literature, search where you will."[5] Staggering, yes . . . but the apparent exclusiveness of it has bothered me, too, until it has dawned on me to ask not only what Jesus is saying, but also what He is *not* saying.

Jesus is not claiming, "No one comes to *God*, except by me." That would count out not only other religions but, for example, the whole great line of Old Testament men of faith: Abraham and Moses, Isaiah and Jeremiah and David. It would be to deny that anyone other than a Christian could know God at all, and that would be a highly questionable claim.

Jesus *is* saying, "He who has seen me has seen *the Father*." He gives God a name by which literally no one in the world had dared to call God before: "*Our Father* who art in heaven. . . ." Even Jewish scholars have sensed that this, finally, is the watershed between Judaism and Christianity: not a God who waits for His erring children to come crawling home but a God who goes out searching, seeking, saving the lost. The God who is Father is a unique picture in Christianity.

An old story tells of a Roman emperor coming triumphantly through the streets of Rome after a victorious campaign. The empress and her family were seated on a little platform and as the emperor came by, his little son, six years old, jumped off the platform, squirmed through the crowd, and was just about to dash into the street when a legionnaire stopped him and picked him up. "You can't go out there," the guard said, "Don't you know that's

76

the emperor?" The child replied, "He may be your emperor but he's my father!"[6]

The New Testament experience is that there is now a whole new relationship with God. Others may call Him by other names, "but He's our Father!"

III

Who is this then? This Palm Sunday one who comes? He is Lord. He reveals the Father. *And third: He inspires love.*

"The same old stuff," you say. But with Jesus it's all new, for the love He inspires in us is the love that also unites Him with His Father. One of His last prayers was for His disciples, ". . . that they may be one, Father, even as we are one. . . ."[7] His unity with the Father is a unity of love, and to that unity He also calls us. "A new commandment I give to you that you love one another . . . . By this all men will know that you are my disciples, if you have love one for another."[8]

Dick Sheppard told somewhere that he was once out on the downs in England on a night of thick unrelieved darkness. He said he felt "the spirit of the universe" closing in around him. Feeling like a soldier lying in no-man's land and hearing footsteps approaching, he wanted to shout, "Friend or foe?"[9] Sometimes the spirit of the universe seems like more than we can stand. We are scarred and broken; our friends and loved ones seem battered to the point of submission. But somehow, in the midst even of that, the New Testament experience is that the principle at the heart of the universe is love.

The world is full of people who hurt . . . the broken hearts, the anguished spirits, the deep regrets, the unfair pains, the sick, the dying, the bereaved, the lonely.

The world is full of people who hurt: their fevered brows need the cooling touch of love. They need to know that someone cares.

God cares. Twenty centuries ago in Palestine, One came "in the name of the Lord" to make that care visible. And ever since, through all the reverberating years, He has depended on people who care to make *His* care visible. The world is full of people who hurt. Their fevered brows can feel the cooling hand of God's love when they feel your hand and mine. "A new commandment I give to you, that you love one another, even as I have loved you."

A composer sat at a piano and played his most recent composition. When he was through, a friend asked, "What are you trying to say? What does it mean?" Without a word, he sat down and played it all the way through again. Had he been able to say what he meant in words, he would not have said it in music.

How shall we explain God's love? Not so much in words, but by listening to the symphony all over again: the birth, the life, the death, the resurrection of the one who "comes in the name of the Lord." In the listening, you will catch the varied harmonies, the crashing dischords, the drumbeat of death . . . but always the melody of love.

Can there be a higher goal for our own lives? In the name of "the one who comes" and for the sake of a hurting world: always the melody of love!

References

1. Matthew 21:10.
2. Matthew 21:9.
3. Barclay, William; *Who Is Jesus?*; p. 15.
4. John 14:6, 9.
5. *Interpreter's Bible*; volume 8; p. 704.
6. Barclay; *op. cit.*; p. 26.
7. John 17:22.
8. John 13:34-35.
9. Quoted in Barclay; *op. cit.*; pp. 34-35.

Because He Lives!
A Sermon for Easter Sunday
Is there life after death?

Matthew 28:1-10; John 14:18-19

In never-never land, there is a very strange country. When the fall of the year comes there and everything is frozen, the words people speak also freeze up. In the spring, when the thaw comes, those words melt and become audible once more.[1]

Suppose, in reality, your words would live again, thawed out in some future's unguarded moment. What a deterrent to words spoken in anger or malice or untruth if we never knew when or where or in whose presence they were going to be thawed out and played back!

Some words, in fact, *do* live again and again. Easter words, for example: "He is not here; for he has risen! . . . Because I live, you will live also!"[2]

Those words come alive and Easter becomes a day of celebration. But even on this day, there are some "hard questions of faith." There is a variety of them that relate to death and to Easter, but they telescope into one: *"Is there life after death?"* Before we are through, we shall be constrained to add a further question, "Is there life *before* death?" We begin, however, with the question of the ages. It is an Easter question: "Is there life after death?"

I

Move toward an answer this way.

Some years ago, a certain scholar became convinced that the plays attributed to William Shakespeare were actually written by another man, Christopher Marlowe. He obtained permission to open Marlowe's tomb, believing that he would find there the original manuscripts of the plays attributed to Shakespeare. He opened the tomb. He was disappointed. There was no evidence there.

We think of another tomb—deep in the side of a hill just out of Jerusalem. Some women went there early one Sunday morning. The body for which they searched was not in the tomb. They were disappointed . . . until the conviction dawned that the One they looked for could of course not be found there: He had risen!

You'll find a dazzling array of Easter and post-Easter stories in the New Testament. They do not agree with each other in their details. At the tomb, for example, there was one angel or there were two men. Jesus' friends touch Him or they are asked not to touch Him. The risen Lord eats and drinks like everyone else or He has a body that can go through locked doors. A dazzling variety! But that's hardly surprising. For it was a dazzling event! The Gospel accounts are humanly and understandably different from each other, but they never disagree about the central fact. When you open your Bible, at whatever page, always search for the central fact. At Easter, the centrality they all affirmed was just this, and overwhelmingly this: *that the Christ who had been killed was alive*!

How it could be so and what the details were depended, as the telling of facts always depends, on to whom you were talking. But that it was so, they all agreed. When, a few years later, the Apostle Paul was doing his writing, he never once talked about an empty tomb, but he talked over and over again about a risen Christ.

It is the New Testament's unshakeable conviction, then, that Jesus lives. *There is life after death because Jesus lives*. It's as simple, yet as profound as that. There is life after death. Why? *Because He lives*!

Now that's a matter of faith, of belief, not of proof. Some rather interesting things have been written that try to come down on the side of proof. Elisabeth Kübler-Ross, who became famous for her work with dying patients, has taken another step. She has said, "I do not simply believe in life after death; I *know* that there is life after death."[3] She has worked with patients who were pronounced dead and then were revived. They describe having been separated from their bodies, floating blissfully above them. Some have talked of hearing a bell, or soft beautiful music, at the moment of death.

Almost all describe the presence of some religious figure. The daughter of the late Lutheran theologian, Dr. Alvin Mattson, has written a book, *Witness from Beyond*. She claims some fifty-five communications from her father since his death in 1970. She says he has described visits with such men of other ages as Martin Luther and Charles Wesley and "the Lord Jesus in all his radiance."[4]

All of that is decidely interesting. The accounts may or may not be true and dependable. But the Christian does not depend on them: we live by faith, a faith that Christ lives.

"Because I live," He says, "you will live also."[5] When we ask our timid question, "Is there life after death?", the Easter faith comes back with a resounding, "Yes!" The "yes" of our life after death is because of the "yes" of His life after death. "In my Father's house are many rooms . . . I go to prepare a place for you . . . Because I live, you will live also!"[6]

Not proof . . . but a faith that vibrates into every corner of our lives! Shortly after the Russian Revolution, the atheist, Bukharin, addressed an anti-God rally. He bombarded Christianity with all the artillery of argument, abuse, and ridicule at his command. He tried to lay the whole Christian faith in ruins at his feet. When he finished there was a long silence . . . until finally a Russian Orthodox priest asked permission to speak. He walked confidently to the platform, but what could he say? How could he possibly pick up the shattered pieces? He stood beside the atheist. The silence grew deeper. Then, following the ancient tradition of the Church, the priest gave the liturgical greeting of Easter, "Christ is risen!" Instinctively, the whole vast assembly rose to its feet, and the reply came back like words frozen for a long winter, thawed out at last: "He is risen indeed!"[7]

Bukharin had no reply. There is none. For when all the argument is over, we still have a faith tremendous, unshaken by the world's assaults, a faith that He is risen, and because He lives, we too shall live!

II

In some such fashion, we may come at the hard question of life after death. The matter cannot be left there, however. Or rather, the matter will not leave us there. For authentic Christian faith,

81

even on Easter, is not exclusively nor even primarily concerned about the hereafter, but about the here. When we have wrestled with our question about life after death, the Risen Lord Himself comes right back at us with another question: Is there life *before* death? Are you living now? Whether or not you want to live forever, are you alive now? "I came," said Jesus, "that you might have life and have it abundantly."[8]

At the 48th Academy Awards ceremony in early 1976, the most eloquent message was a silent one. Louise Fletcher, accepting the award for Best Actress of the Year, flashed a message in sign language to her deaf parents: "Thank you for teaching me to have a dream." The dream of Easter is not only about life after death but about the true abundance of our lives before death.

An American journalist once visited Dr. Albert Schweitzer. He came away saying, "Here is a man who lives completely." One of our hymns has us sing,

> "New every morning is the love
> Our wakening and uprising prove. . . ."[9]

Each new morning is a gift of God's compassion, but with each rising of the sun, there is also a question. It is addressed to those who would live life completely and not let it disappear in little snippets. The question is: In this new day of God's love, what will my love show? When the sun is not rising but sinking in some golden hue of the West, shall I have done anything that justifies naming myself a Christian? In the name of the One who lived and lives and lives forever, have I lived completely?

Henry David Thoreau said one time, "I went to the woods because I wished to live deliberately, to front only the essential facts of life, and see if I could not learn what it had to teach, and *not*, when I came to die, discover that I had not lived."[10] Jesus said, "I came so you could live, and live abundantly . . . Because I live, you too shall live!" It's life after death, and it's life before death! Life, not only for ourselves, but on behalf of the Living Christ, life for the sake of others!

On television in England some time ago there was a series of programs entitled "Man Seeking God." An interviewer, Christopher Mayhew by name, talked with representatives of the major religions. He asked how they found God. A Moslem took him to the mosque at prayer time. A Hindu showed him the ritual of sacrifice in the temple. A Jew read to him from the prophets. And a Christian took him to a home for lepers! In those hopeless, twisted, scarred faces he saw the beauty of Christ!

The faces of the world stare at us—from earth's remotest corners and from next door; from across the town and from our own living rooms. They are hopeless faces and scared ones, anxious and distressed, perplexed and grieving, lovely and loveless. In them, each of them, we see the face of Christ. And in us, each of us, they wonder if they will be able to see the fabulous, fantastic truth of Easter . . . the truth that because He lives, we too are alive! The words, frozen by the long, cold journey of Lent and life, vibrate in our ears once more: "Because I live, you too shall live!"

We may believe that there is life after death! But the first question is: Are you alive before death?

References

1. From the tales of Antiphanes of Bergen.
2. Matthew 28:6; John 14:19.
3. Quoted in *Christian Century*; April 14, 1976; p. 363.
4. Quoted in *Minneapolis Star*; April 3, 1976; p. 10A.
5. John 14:19.
6. John 14:2, 19.
7. Newbigin, Lesslie; *A Faith for this One World?*; pp. 59–60.
8. John 10:10.
9. *The Methodist Hymnal*; No. 499.
10. Thoreau, Henry David, *Walden*.

Let Us Pray

Quiet stirrings within us remind us of a great God beyond us. The tug of duty, the tremor of loyalty, the ties of compassion all point us to a glory above our grubbiness. That glory is divine! It comes with Spirit-hand to touch our earth-bound hurts. So our throbbing foreheads are cooled and our racing hearts are calmed. In quiet confidence, we turn to One who said, "Set your troubled hearts at rest!"

Amen!

CONCLUSION

God Is God, No Matter What

Psalm 90:1-4

Here is a word of strength for you: *God is God, no matter what.*

The cover of *Time* magazine one Christmastime all too appropriately captured the mood of America. A bedraggled, befuddled, benumbed and skinny Santa Claus was dragging a patched and empty bag behind him. An hour with the evening paper or the 10:00 p.m. news is enough to make us want to burn the paper or push our foot through the tube. We aren't sure we can stand any more! We're like the fellow who read that smoking was bad for his health, so he decided to give up reading! We'd like to shut our eyes and pretend all the bad news is just not there!

The affirmation of the Bible, however, is that you can look it all straight in the eye! All those "turmoils without, within" can be stared down with a final confidence. Why? Not because you and I are either strong or weak, but because God is God . . . no matter what!

I

A

Think back to the Old Testament. Here, for example, is the Book of Job with all its anguish. We talk about the patience of Job, but that just shows we haven't read it very thoroughly. The man went through hell and he shook his fist at God about it. We can vibrate with him. We understand him. Some days, a hundred agonized

87

heartaches make us want to do our own fist-shaking. But is there not something beautiful about the fact that so tortured a story is followed immediately by the Book of Psalms? There must have been some method in the madness of the people who decided on that order. Perhaps, indeed, that madness was divine! For here, following all the tortured agonies of Job, we have time and again the outcries of confidence. Listen to the eighth Psalmist:

"O Lord, our Lord, how majestic is thy name in all the earth!"

Or the twenty-third:

"The Lord is my shepherd; I shall not want!"

Or the forty-sixth:

"God is our refuge and strength, a very present help in trouble."

Or the ninetieth Psalm makes a great affirmation which we may take out and fasten on the clothesline of our attention:

"Lord, thou hast been our dwelling place in all generations.
Before the mountains were brought forth,
    or ever thou hadst formed the earth and the world,
    from everlasting to everlasting thou art God."

B

"From everlasting to everlasting . . . ." We could get into a fantastically complicated philosophical discussion about that. We could tickle our brains for a very long time, trying to define eternity and infinity. Many philosphers and theologians have done so. But a finely honed definition was not the Psalmist's goal. It need not be our purpose. Instead, with that ancient writer, we can make a great affirmation. It is this: farther back and farther forward than we can begin to imagine, God has been involved and will be involved. The *Gloria Patri* says it:

"Glory be to the Father, and to the Son, and to the Holy Ghost, As it was in the beginning, is now, and ever shall be, World without end!"

Or to put it even more succinctly: "From everlasting to everlasting, God is God, no matter what!"

88

II

A

During the last week of November in 1974, a team of American scientists in Puerto Rico, believing there is life elsewhere in the universe, beamed a message to a cluster of stars in the Milky Way. Traveling at the speed of light—186,000 miles per second—it will take 24,000 years for the message to arrive at its destination and (if anyone is listening) 24,000 years for a reply to return!

Such is the magnitude of even the discernible universe. Yet the breath-taking declaration of our faith is that the God who has reached to the farthest star of the Milky Way will put His cooling hand on your throbbing forehead! He reaches there and yet His everlasting arms support you when you're too tired to stand.

From everlasting to everlasting . . . God is God, no matter what!

B

Up in Northwestern Minnesota there's a magnificent slice of creation called Palmer Lake. My family and I say we bought a little of it a few years back. Actually, the good Lord (who made it aeons ago) still owns it, but He's letting us use it for a while. Standing on its shore one cool summer evening, a billion stars and a sliver of moon reflecting on the mirror-like still water, and having myself retreated from a week of more "hecticity" than usual, I thought to myself, "Who cares about those issues that have been tying me in knots?"

Well, of course, we need to care about the issues of our lives. But the still and quiet grandeur of that evening put my inner churnings into a quite different perspective. For there had been a thousand thousand evenings there before, and it was a little easier to believe that all would be well, and that if I had done my best, that was enough. For beyond our best all that finally counts is that from everlasting to everlasting, God is God, no matter what!

C

Lord Salisbury, the British Prime Minister under Queen Victoria, used to advise students of foreign affairs to use "large maps."[2] He wanted the crisis of some small corner to be seen in a larger view. Someone else has wisely advised that we stand still and listen to what the centuries say to the years.

From everlasting to everlasting, God is God, no matter what!

D

The New Testament comes to us with the same kind of message. It is a word of sublime confidence. Here, for example, is Jesus in the Sermon on the Mount:

> "Look at the birds of the air: they neither sow nor reap nor gather into barns and yet your heavenly Father feeds them . . . Consider the lilies of the field, how they grow; they neither toil nor spin . . . and if God so clothes the grass of the field, will he not much more clothe you, O men of little faith?"[3]

There it is in a nutshell? "O men of little faith!" Is He not asking us to recall our true foundations? Is He not pleading with us to remember the things that ultimately count? To stare everything else down, and to take hold of the quiet resource of confidence in the Creator? Is He not urging us, with all the intensity of His own faith, to grab hold of the conviction that God is God, no matter what—and never let go of it? And then does not the heart of the Apostle Paul beat in tune with the heart of the Master when he looks at everything that can possibly happen to us and exults:

> ". . . neither death, nor life, nor angels, nor principalities, nor things present, nor things to come . . . nor anything else in all creation will be able to separate us from the love of God in Christ Jesus our Lord."[4]

From everlasting to everlasting . . . God is God, no matter what!

E

A few years ago, some granite rocks were found near Redwood Falls in Minnesota. They proved to be the oldest rocks ever analyzed anywhere. They go back some four billion years; that is, to within 500 million years of the estimated birth of the planet itself . . . give or take a month or two!

God was making Minnesota four billion years ago! And twenty

or forty or eighty years ago, or whatever, He created you. He cares for Minnesota . . . and for every corner of His earth anywhere . . . He cares for you. For we believe that farther back and farther forward than we can begin to imagine, God has been involved and will be involved. Isaac Watts' stately hymn captures it:

> "Before the hills in order stood,
> Or earth received her frame,
> From everlasting thou art God,
> To endless years the same.
>
> O God, our help in ages past,
> Our hope for years to come,
> Be thou our guide while life shall last,
> And our eternal home!"[5]

Hold on to this, then: *From everlasting to everlasting, God is God —no matter what!*

References

1. *Time*; December 2, 1974; p. 12.
2. *Interpreter's Bible*; volume 4; p. 56.
3. Matthew 6:26, 28, 30.
4. Romans 8:38-39.
5. *Methodist Hymnal*; No. 28; Stanzas 3 and 6.

Let Us Pray

You have promised to be with me, Lord, but this loneliness of mine is pretty hard to take. There are lots of people, but they all seem so busy, so happy. They have friends. And if they turn to me, I wonder if it's only because they feel sorry. Then the aloneness is more painful than ever. Do You understand my cry? You must, for Jesus was left so alone. In the midst of my isolation, then, I begin to understand everyone feels this sometimes. And the truth glimmers in the horizon of my soul: "Emmanuel" means You are here. So help me to reach to others, and to accept them reaching for me. All in Your Spirit!

Emmanuel! Amen!